EISENHOWER BABIES

RONNIE BLAIR

EISENHOWER BABIES

GROWING UP ON **MOONSHOTS, COMIC BOOKS,** AND **BLACK-AND-WHITE TV**

Published by Advantage, Charleston, South Carolina.
Member of Advantage Media.

ADVANTAGE is a registered trademark, and the Advantage colophon is a trademark of Advantage Media Group, Inc.

Printed in the United States of America.

10 9 8 7 6 5 4 3 2 1

ISBN: 978-1-64225-542-3 (Paperback)
ISBN: 978-1-64225-541-6 (eBook)

LCCN: 2022918682

Book design by Analisa Smith.

This publication is designed to provide accurate and authoritative information in regard to the subject matter covered. It is sold with the understanding that the publisher is not engaged in rendering legal, accounting, or other professional services. If legal advice or other expert assistance is required, the services of a competent professional person should be sought.

Advantage Media helps busy entrepreneurs, CEOs, and leaders write and publish a book to grow their business and become the authority in their field. Advantage authors comprise an exclusive community of industry professionals, idea-makers, and thought leaders. Do you have a book idea or manuscript for consideration? We would love to hear from you at **AdvantageMedia.com**.

To my wife, Carol, and my sons, Alex and Andy

CONTENTS

PREFACE 1

CHAPTER 1 5
In the Shadow of Black Mountain

CHAPTER 2 11
Hoot Gibson, Red Man Tobacco, and My Father

CHAPTER 3 17
Bedtime Prayers, Seventeen Little Bears, and My Mother

CHAPTER 4 23
The Valley of the Poor Fork of the Cumberland

CHAPTER 5 31
A Hoosier Interlude

CHAPTER 6 35
The Houses That Built Me

CHAPTER 7 43
Sixteen Tons—and Then Some

CHAPTER 8 49
Dad Goes to War

CHAPTER 9 59
Rodney

CHAPTER 10 61
The Alligator Next Door

CHAPTER 11 65
I Borrow a Pony

CHAPTER 12 69
Purple-Ink Journalism, Supreme Court Rulings,
and Other School Happenings

CHAPTER 13 77
Mickey Mouse, King Kong,
and Other Thirty-Five-Cent Celluloid Escapades

CHAPTER 14 81
The Church That Bore My Family Name

CHAPTER 15 85
Space Ghost Goes Trick-or-Treating

CHAPTER 16 89
Nights before Christmas, Shepherd Mishaps,
and a Missing Johnny Seven

CHAPTER 17 97
Thrilling Trips and Backseat Nausea

CHAPTER 18 103
Brought to You by Kellogg's—
and a Cable Antenna atop Black Mountain

CHAPTER 19 107
Roy Rogers, a Battered Broom, and Me

CHAPTER 20 111
The Supermarket That Swallowed a Baseball Field

CHAPTER 21 115
The Architect, the Engineer, and the Mumps

CHAPTER 22 119
Hanna-Barbera, Saturday Mornings,
and a Boston Mother Who Ruined Everything

CHAPTER 23 123
The Case of the Relentless Reader

CHAPTER 24 131
The World Intrudes

CHAPTER 25 137
Dear Comic Book Editor

CHAPTER 26 143
The Homesick Trumpeter Blues

CHAPTER 27 149
Coal Mine, Moonshine, or Move it on Down the Line

ACKNOWLEDGMENTS 155

BIBLIOGRAPHY 159

ABOUT THE AUTHOR 163

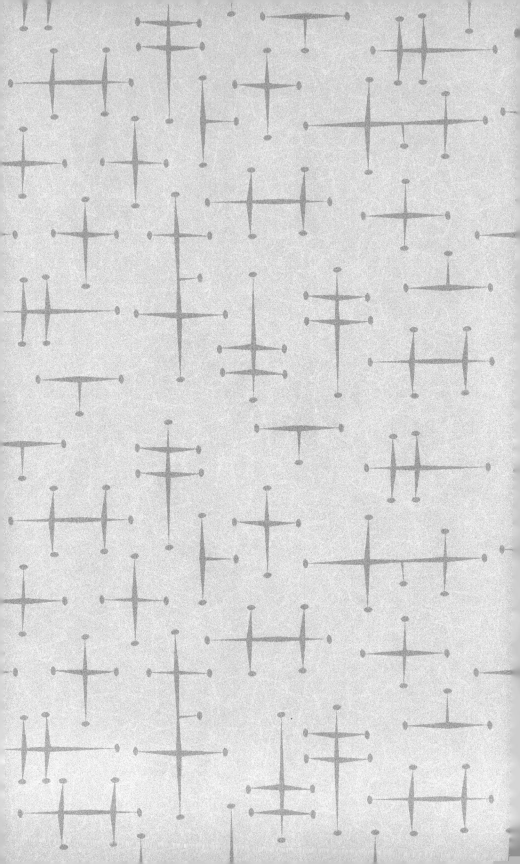

PREFACE

Many childhood memoirs revolve around trauma: alcoholic fathers, clinically depressed mothers, a life-changing tragedy that must be overcome despite extraordinary odds.

I do not have that to offer.

Many tales set in Appalachia, as this one is, play on stereotypes: hillbillies with guns, hillbillies with moonshine stills, hillbillies baffled by the simplest of modern technology.

I do not have that to offer either.

Sure, in these pages you will detect an occasional hint of Kentucky's hillbilly history, but even in the 1960s it was difficult to maintain much Li'l Abner ignorance about the world when you were watching *Voyage to the Bottom of the Sea* on TV, following the exploits of Apollo astronauts, and reading twelve-cent Spider-Man comic books.

Yes, pretty much what every other kid across America was doing at the same time.

Adults, of course, were appalled at us, especially with our TV-watching habits, which they worried would stunt our intellectual and physical growth, not to mention destroy our eyesight if we sat too close to the screen. It was as if adults of the era saw TV as a strange malevolent beast invading their homes, even though it was they who opened the front door and gave the beast a grand welcome. In 1968, a *Time* magazine article explored the TV addiction of ten-year-old youngsters like me and quoted one education expert who predicted doom for our entire generation: "Kids come into school today and they wait for people to tell them things. Without handling frogs or flying a kite, they lead less of a life. We're moving along in a mold that will produce people I can't even imagine."

These words could have proved soul crushing, but we were too busy handling frogs and flying kites to take notice. Of course, that educator was part of a proud apocalyptic tradition among adults fretting about the habits of wayward youth. A little over a decade earlier, psychiatrist Fredric Wertham wrote a book titled *Seduction of the Innocent* in which he swore it was villainous comic books that would lead to an entire generation's demise. Around the same time, Rudolf Flesch wrote the bestseller *Why Johnny Can't Read* in which he led the nation in mourning what a sad lot of illiterates schools were producing by teaching children to read through the "look say" method popular in Dick and Jane books.

Adults hyperventilated. We kids marched confidently into the future, which one of our TV shows, *The Jetsons*, promised would involve flying cars and robot maids. Adults really just needed to calm down.

So, if not family trauma or hillbilly burlesque that could have erupted from a Ma and Pa Kettle movie, what do these pages offer?

You will find various pinches and dashes of nostalgia, history, geography, popular culture, and everyday human foibles and heart-aches. Perhaps you also will be reminded that the past does not represent more innocent times, as we so often hear, but instead that most of us were more innocent during those times. Adults bore the burden of worrying about assassinations, wars, and labor disputes. We kids built forts, fielded fly balls with a Willie Mays signature glove, and pedaled furiously down neighborhood roads on psychedelically painted banana-seat bicycles.

That some of us did this in California or Maine while others did it in the back hills of Kentucky seemed to make minimal difference. This does not mean that all of our experiences were exactly the same. I didn't ride the subway, and New York City kids didn't watch mules plow fields. But in post–World War II America, and definitely by the 1960s, geography had lost some of its power to isolate us. Those who lived in tiny southeastern Kentucky communities like mine were no longer "marooned on an island of mountains," which is the way author James Watt Raine put it in his 1924 book *The Land of Saddle-Bags: A Study of the Mountain People of Appalachia*. In Raine's view, "passable roads" were our ticket to sociological progress, but the introduction of radio and especially television also played a pivotal role. Raine was just writing too early to know that.

At its essence, *Eisenhower Babies* is about a time and a place that are no more but that also never went away as long as any child can daydream about heroic exploits on horseback, scan Christmas Eve skies for evidence of flying reindeer, explore libraries for vicarious adventures, and wonder what new magic lies a day or two away.

CHAPTER 1

IN THE SHADOW OF BLACK MOUNTAIN

Older kids told us the tale with the smug superiority that comes with a couple of years' head start in elementary school. If you crossed Black Mountain on a night when the fog lay so thick that even the brightest headlights couldn't penetrate it, you would encounter Headless Annie. She would emerge from the thick woods, a malevolent being bent on ...

On what, exactly?

We had questions.

Why was she headless?

Did she carry her head, or was she looking for it?

What would she do if she had us in her clutches?

How does an apparition go about getting you in her clutches, anyway?

The answers lacked clarity. The older kids had limits to their knowledge, despite their advanced years. Depending on who told the tale, Annie had lost her head in a car accident at the foot of the mountain. Or maybe it had happened during Harlan County's violent coal mine wars of the 1930s, when Annie's father angered the wrong people and they sought revenge. Or maybe the beheading had happened by means best left unstated lest some curse fall upon you because of your familiarity with the revealed truth.

The vagueness surrounding her origin just added to Headless Annie's mystique.

We didn't believe, anyway—not really—though on the rare nights when a trip home to Kentucky from Virginia required a late-night drive across Black Mountain, I searched the darkness, fearful she would appear yet also yearning for a sighting.

Headless Annie remained hidden from view, refusing to expose herself. That was fine. Black Mountain, the highest point in Kentucky at 4,145 feet, was imposing enough without the need for a supernatural overseer, headless or otherwise. My father would drive on into the darkness, concerned more with safely navigating the curvy, narrow road than with eluding spirits from the land of the dead. Those worries he left to his son, who remained alert in his backseat perch, prepared to sound the alarm about the looming threat should Annie materialize.

"You almost lost her, didn't you, Doctor?"

The nurse likely didn't intend for my mother to hear those words, but as she hovered on the edge of consciousness, she did hear them, and the nurse's somber question heralded my arrival into the world.

I was a breech baby, my birth problematic for both my mother and the doctor—and I suppose for me as well. At the time, a breech baby was as much as twenty times more likely to die than the average newborn, so it was a dicey beginning. Happily, things got better after that, and while I was not the perfect child, to which my mother would have attested, I at least kept the drama to a minimum. Well, there was that alarming incident with the wasps and another one with a rattle-snake. But if you don't count those, and you don't count the barn loft catastrophe or the death-defying pedal car disaster, then things went smoothly and only a dozen or so of my mother's eventual gray hairs could be traced directly to me. Two dozen, tops.

> **While I was not the perfect child, to which my mother would have attested, I at least kept the drama to a minimum.**

But back to my awkward entrance into the world, which came about on a January night in 1958 in Lynch, Kentucky, a coal-mining community that lies in the shadow of Black Mountain.

My parents were Ellison Blair and Jeanette Scott Blair, a couple whose lives had been defined by the Great Depression, World War II, and the death of their first son from a congenital heart condition. A big sister, two-and-a-half-year-old Shelia, awaited my arrival, and a couple of years later a little brother, Ricky, joined us.

This was a time that many Americans look back on with nostalgia, proclaiming it perhaps the most perfect era of middle-class bliss in the nation's history. Others beg to differ, insisting that behind the facade was a nation whose troubles were simmering uncontrollably and would boil over into the protests of the 1960s. Many people, it seemed, came to confuse the flawed real world of the 1950s with the fictional version portrayed on popular TV shows such as *The Adventures of Ozzie and Harriet.*

The president was grandfatherly Dwight D. Eisenhower, the World War II general who successfully made the transition to civilian politician. I have no memory of his presidency, yet over time I came to think of Shelia, Ricky, and me, along with most of the childhood friends we played with, as Eisenhower Babies because of his role as the nation's leader at the time we burst into the world as part of the baby boom. The baby boom straddled four administrations—from Harry Truman in 1946 to Lyndon B. Johnson in 1964—but Eisenhower Babies arrived in some of the boom's most prolific years. The number of annual births topped four million in eleven of the boom years. The US Census Bureau reports that seven of those eleven years fell during Eisenhower's presidency.

At the time of my birth, the union consisted of forty-eight states. Alaska and Hawaii would not join until the next year. World War II was only thirteen years in the past, the Space Age was just getting started, and young people had added the cha-cha to their dance floor moves. On the other side of the world, future martial arts film star Bruce Lee was crowned the 1958 Hong Kong Cha-Cha Champion.

Of course, these are all things I learned later. As with most people, my first years are a blank, though not without significant milestones, because I did learn to walk, talk, and come to understand where I fell among family relationships. But then September 1960 arrived, my mother gave birth to my brother, Ricky, and my consciousness started to crystallize. I was a mere two and a half years old, so I can only guess that the memory became embedded because it was such a momentous occasion. Shelia and I stayed with an aunt and uncle while Mom delivered our little brother, and after the hospital discharged her, we hopped into the back seat of the car for the drive home. I leaned forward to get a good look at the baby, whom Mom held in her arms in the front seat. Infant seats in cars were still a couple of years away from existing and a couple of decades away from becoming mandatory.

"What's his name, again?" I asked.

"Ricky," Mom said.

A mile or two passed.

"What's his name, again?" Apparently, at two and a half I already suffered from short-term memory loss.

"Ricky," Mom said patiently.

The car came to a stop at the house we rented, and the five of us went inside. I was now a big brother. It was my first promotion.

CHAPTER 2

HOOT GIBSON, RED MAN TOBACCO, AND MY FATHER

I rarely heard my father discuss politics, other than to mention that his mother had become so incensed with Herbert Hoover that she vowed to never vote for a Republican again, a declaration that wounded my GOP-leaning grandfather immensely.

So, it was surprising one day in the early 1970s when my father and one of my uncles became involved in a heated exchange about a topic simmering in the news.

The topic was the military draft. Should the United States have one, or should the nation require the armed forces to rely on volunteers? In this living room version of point-counterpoint, my uncle expounded on the virtues of a draft and the benefits of thrusting young men into service to their country whether they preferred to serve or not. My father championed the antidraft position, contending that plucking reluctant eighteen-year-olds from their homes and sending them overseas with rifles served neither the nation nor the young men.

If their debate sounds like an academic exercise today, it's critical to note that at the time the Vietnam War was in its final throes and the draft a real concern looming over the nation's youth. My father and uncle's debate had this added element: they were both World War II veterans, yet their experiences had led them to diametrically opposed positions on this particular military question.

Each refused to concede ground, and eventually my uncle left in a red-faced huff.

My father stood in the doorway, watching him drive away.

"He has daughters," Dad said. "If he had sons, he would have a different opinion."

My father, Ellison Blair, was born on January 10, 1920, just fourteen months after the armistice that ended World War I. On that day, it was far too soon to guess that Dad would someday fight in a second war that would envelop nearly the entire planet or that over time he would cultivate such impassioned antidraft sentiments.

Dad was part of a large family, so he had ready-made playmates, and his parents, Gillis and Rossie Blair, had ample hands to help with chores. As a boy, Dad hired himself out to neighbors, chopping wood or taking on other work in exchange for a dime—the price of a ticket at the local movie theater. At the time, Westerns were popular and B-movie cowboys reigned. Stars such as Ken Maynard and Tom Mix rode their way across the West in black-and-white films in which good triumphed over evil in ninety minutes or less.

Dad's favorite of these B-movie cowboys was Hoot Gibson, a rodeo star who'd stumbled into silent films when a director sought experienced cowboys for a 1910 movie titled *Pride of the Range*. It would be ten years before Gibson started getting lead roles, but from the 1920s to the 1940s, he held dominion as one of the top box office draws among Western stars. Like many children, Dad appreciated the comedic touch that Hoot Gibson brought to the Western-movie genre at a time when other cowboys were dead serious.

Western novels failed to captivate Dad in the same way as the movies. He sampled the works of Zane Grey but grew frustrated by Grey's excruciatingly detailed descriptions of the Western landscape. In the movies, Dad could see that landscape without the need for long-winded prose about slopes that "descended to a dim line of cañons from which rose an up-flinging of the earth, not mountainous, but a vast heave of purple uplands, with ribbed and fan-shaped walls, castle-crowned cliffs, and gray escarpments."

After attempting to gallop through this lush verbiage, my father decided to stick with film as his preferred venue for tales of cowboy derring-do.

Although Dad moved out of the Kentucky mountains on a few occasions—for army service in the 1940s and for much-needed employment in Indiana and Maryland after that—he always returned to Harlan County, his birthplace and childhood home. Like many men in the area, he found gainful employment in the coal mines, working his way into a position as a shuttle-car driver for a mine owned by US Steel.

Shuttle cars hauled freshly mined coal from the mine face and deposited it on a conveyor belt, where the coal would then be swept out of the mine. Although it was critical to the enterprise, the shuttle-car driver's job was tediously repetitive. Pick up coal at the face, and take it to the belt. Return to the face and repeat, over and over for eight monotonous hours. Through much of my childhood, Dad worked the second shift, which began at 4:00 p.m. and ended at midnight. That meant we saw little of him on workdays, especially once we reached school age, because his sleeping schedule and ours were not in sync.

In his free time, Dad followed University of Kentucky sports, sitting beside a large black radio to listen to the play-by-play for football and basketball games that only infrequently were televised at the time. He cheered the Wildcats' victories and grumbled at their losses, the latter of which were occasional for the talented basketball team but routine for the luckless football team. Dad cautioned me to refrain from celebrating a Kentucky touchdown or even a first down before giving the play-by-play announcer ample time to intone, "There's a flag on the play."

Although Dad did not drink or smoke, he did engage in one unhealthy habit. He chewed tobacco, and pouches of Red Man could usually be found around our house. Ever the frugal Depression-era child, Dad cut off the bottom portion of a milk carton to serve as a spittoon rather than buy a brass or porcelain one.

Somewhat out of character, Dad enjoyed sensational true crime magazines such as *Startling Detective* and *True Detective*. Lurid headlines screamed out from their covers. "Would Her Severed Fingers Point to Her Killer?" "How He Butchered the New York Beauties." Inside the magazines, the articles didn't quite live up to the headlines. Yes, they provided graphic crime details usually glossed over in family-friendly newspapers. But beyond that they were nonfiction police procedurals. Since they were lying around the house, I tried to read these magazines, but they failed to entice me the way the more atmospheric crime fiction in *Alfred Hitchcock's Mystery Magazine* did, so I kept my allegiance with Mr. Hitchcock.

On occasion, when I ventured into town to buy comic books at the Rexall drugstore, Dad would ask me to pick up a couple of the magazines, likely raising the eyebrows of the prim and proper middle-aged women at the cash register when I plunked down a shockingly gruesome cover of *Crime Detective* alongside a copy of *Detective Comics* featuring Batman. Although when you think about it, is a cover with a blurb that reads "Five Minutes to Kill: Slaughter Spree of the Random Robber" really that distinct from a cover with a blurb that reads "Batman Challenges the Reader to Guess ... Who Is the Killer in the Smog?"

Either way, while Dad's reading habits may have leaned toward the sensational, his demeanor was much more dull. His idea of an exciting evening out was to take us to the drive-in for ice cream cones or to visit relatives and chat about old times over decaffeinated coffee. This was fine, because although 1960s kids might have wished for exotic fathers in the James Bond mode, what we really needed were practical men who could dish out advice, spare change, or chewing gum as the moment and circumstances required.

> **Although 1960s kids might have wished for exotic fathers in the James Bond mode, what we really needed were practical men who could dish out advice, spare change, or chewing gum as the moment and circumstances required.**

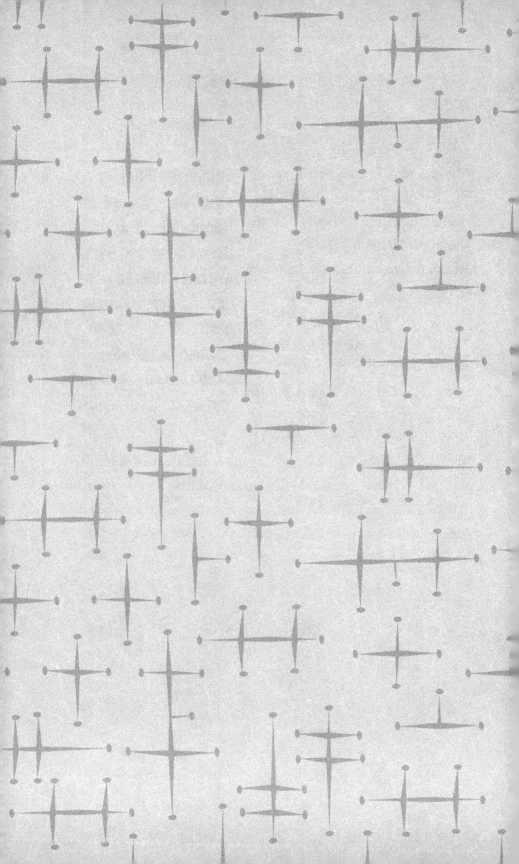

CHAPTER 3

BEDTIME PRAYERS, SEVENTEEN LITTLE BEARS, AND MY MOTHER

Each evening as my brother, sister, and I clambered into our beds, my mother posed a question.

"Did you say your prayers?"

She was a stickler for this, but at least she did not expect us to come up with a brand-new nightly prayer begging for forgiveness for our failings or pleading with God to make a Flintstones coloring book magically appear by morning. Instead, she taught us the tried-and-true children's bedtime prayer that we could dash off in haste:

> *Now I lay me down to sleep,*
> *I pray the Lord my soul to keep,*
> *If I should die before I wake,*
> *I pray the Lord my soul to take.*

It's a morbid prayer when you think about it, but I didn't. I said it quickly by rote, zipping through the "if I should die" part with such speed that it came out sounding like one mysterious word—*ifashadie*. If nothing else, the prayer was less gloomy that way, and Mom never cautioned me to slow down lest God become confused about what message I was trying to convey. She would walk away pleased that, as I drifted off to sleep, I was still in good standing with the Heavenly Father.

My mother was born Jeanette Scott on October 20, 1923, to parents William and Mary Ann Scott, and like Dad, she was part of a large family that in her case included a couple of half sisters from her father's first marriage. They lived in the tiny community of Blair, Kentucky, where Mom and her siblings were surrounded by nature and where, on winter days, a potbellied stove heated their two-room school.

It was perhaps on one of those winter days that Mom became enthralled with *The Seventeen Little Bears*, by Laura Rountree Smith, a book she discovered in the school library. She devoured each word, possibly more than once. Certainly it captivated her enough that she would remember the book with fondness the rest of her life.

When she was in her seventies, Mom became obsessed with tracking down her old childhood storybook companion, but she couldn't recall the author, and the title meant nothing to librarians in the 1990s. The book also refused to turn up in internet searches, until one day around 1999 or 2000 I stumbled across a copy for sale online in an antiquarian bookstore in California. I ordered *The Seventeen Little Bears* and mailed the book to Mom, who was joyful at finally being reunited with this old friend from childhood. She devoured it once again, admitting, though, that nothing about the cover, the story, or the illustrations sparked any recognition. What had stayed with her over the decades had simply been the book's title and the delight she experienced as a little girl who had discovered the power of a good story.

Whether for lack of interest or lack of opportunity, Mom didn't learn to drive as a young woman, which created problems for her when Dad went off to work, leaving her alone with three small children who might be in need of emergency medical care at any moment. At some point in the early to mid-1960s, likely tired of taxis, walking, and a semi-isolated existence, she decided enough was enough.

"I'm getting a driver's license," she said.

Dad gave Mom her first tentative driving lessons in front of the house we rented, the car easing slowly down the street as she accustomed herself to the unfamiliar driver's seat after decades as a passenger. Several weeks later she took her driver's test, and the government decreed her qualified. My mother's insistence on getting that driver's license gave her a freedom she did not have before. Now she could, on a whim, visit friends on the far edge of town, gather with her quilting-bee buddies, or embark on an impromptu shopping excursion. But she placed self-imposed limits on how far she would travel; no crossing Black Mountain or roaring down interstates for her, thank you very much. She rarely if ever drove more than six or seven miles from the house.

By the time all three of us were in elementary school, Mom had taken on two part-time jobs. One was at a second-hand clothing store operated by Save the Children Federation, an organization started in England in 1919 as the Save the Children Fund. When the Depression hit, a group of people in the United States decided the organization could do some good on our shores, and in 1932 they launched the American version, providing underprivileged children with clothes, shoes, books, and toys.

Mom's boss at the Save the Children Federation store (which we referred to as simply Save the Children) was Ada Cornett, who lived outside of town. Mrs. Cornett had a fish pond on her property where Shelia, Ricky, and I once caught a large haul of fish using cane poles, worms, and all the luck we could muster. Mrs. Cornett came to know us well because the three of us often walked into town after school and hung out in the store until closing.

But keeping young children entertained in a used-clothing store proved a challenge, so Mom was relieved when one of her friends, who lived in a second-floor apartment across the street, offered to let us come over and watch afternoon cartoons.

On some days, when our hair became too unruly for Mom's taste, Ricky and I walked a block or two down the street to a barber shop for a haircut. Next door was the Rexall drugstore, which sold twelve-cent comic books. Sometimes I would go in there, browsing through the latest issues of *Action Comics*, *House of Mystery*, *The Brave and the Bold*, and other titles before choosing something to take back to Save the Children. I would hide away in the rear of the store and read, blocking out the monotony of the afternoon as Superman battled his latest outmatched foe.

One perk of working at the store was that Mom helped unpack shipments of clothing and had first dibs on anything that might fit one of us. She sifted through the deliveries like a prospector panning for gold, gleefully pouncing on a shirt for me, a pair of pants for Ricky, or a dress for Shelia. For a few years, our wardrobes consisted largely of the finest in used clothing that Save the Children could provide.

Mom's other part-time job in the 1960s was as a waitress at the ironically named Modern Café, an old-fashioned mom-and-pop restaurant owned by an older couple, Madge and Tom Deal. The restaurant was in that same stretch of businesses, less than a minute's walk from Save the Children. The Modern Café had a few booths, a few tables, and a long counter with stools you could spin around on until a frowning adult put a halt to your revelry. I came to know all the waitresses—mostly middle-aged women like Mom—and on occasion when I dropped in near the end of Mom's shift, Madge Deal prepared a grilled cheese sandwich for me, no charge.

Mom's waitressing job included tips, so on those days she arrived home with a jingling array of coins. Many of those coins ended up in our possession. On school mornings, Mom set out a dime and three pennies for each of us. This amount was not random. Our school had a morning break when we could purchase small cartons of chocolate milk for three cents. The school also had an afternoon break when students could line up at a soda machine that dispensed drinks in plastic cups for a dime. Occasionally, the soda machine

As befitted a woman raised in the Kentucky mountains, my mother had a few colorful sayings at the ready.

misfired and the plastic cup failed to drop into position. We would watch in dismay as our precious soda sprayed out and, with nothing to catch it, disappeared down a drain.

As befitted a woman raised in the Kentucky mountains, my mother had a few colorful sayings at the ready and would entertain us with her Appalachian wit and wisdom. Always aware that the possibility of unforeseen circumstances lurked, she hedged her promises with a caveat: "Lord willing and the creek don't rise." If another adult displayed a lack of sound reasoning, she would pronounce her judgment: "He ain't got the sense God gave a goose."

Like many parents in the mountains in those days, Mom and Dad believed in punishing children with a few lashes from a switch. If Mom had to handle this regrettable chore, she carefully avoided switching us right before supper lest we, in our misery, lose our appetites. Much like a broom or a mop, a switch was just one more household tool, assigned to a corner or a shelf until needed. My parents refrained from pulling out the switch for minor or one-time offenses. They resorted to it only after the third, fourth, or eleventh warning.

Although Mom did not speak about it often, one regret she had was that she did not finish high school. In 1930s Kentucky, with the Depression in full swing, many families came to view school as a luxury and thought their children's time would be better spent earning extra money for the family or assisting with gardening or other chores. It did not help that high school students had to pay for their own textbooks, a situation particularly problematic for parents with eight or nine children. After ninth grade, Mom reluctantly dropped out and devoted those hours previously used for schooling to helping her family survive. Dad had done the same even earlier, in eighth grade.

You would think, considering my father never attended high school at all and my mother for only one year, that their dream would be to see their children earn high school diplomas.

That was not the case.

Instead, they instilled in us a much more ambitious message: "You will go to college."

CHAPTER 4

THE VALLEY OF THE POOR FORK OF THE CUMBERLAND

The magnificent 688-mile-long Cumberland River begins humbly in Harlan County, Kentucky, where three major forks merge into one to form the river's headwaters. Two of those forks are Martin's Fork and Clover Fork. The third—and most important to me—is the forty-five-mile-long Poor Fork. It is in the valley of the Poor Fork of the Cumberland River that I was born and raised.

My hometown is in fact called Cumberland, stealing its identity from the river. But Cumberland, with a population of roughly forty-two hundred when I was born, did not always go by such an illustrious name.

Instead, when the community was settled in 1837, the town seers bestowed upon it the less-than-noble name of Poor Fork, Kentucky. The name made sense geographically but lacked a proper level of dignity. Eventually, community leaders saw the error of the town founders' ways and in the 1920s changed the name to Cumberland, declaring in a resolution that Poor Fork was "unbecoming to a community with the industry and progressiveness now displayed in and around said town."

Although those community leaders elected to grace the town itself with a respectable no-nonsense name, they left room for more creativity when it came to neighborhoods and landmarks, such as Sawmill Holler, Sanctified Hill, Raven's Rock, and Looney Creek. The townspeople clearly could conjure memorable names when they put their minds to it.

Cumberland's economy depended on coal mining, and each day trains hauled coal out of our community to parts unknown—at least unknown to me. Train tracks crisscrossed the town, and traffic on the main streets would come to a halt as train cars rumbled past with mounds of coal peeking out from their open tops. My parents waited patiently through these interruptions, but I fidgeted anxiously in the back seat until the welcome sight of the caboose appeared. When no trains were in sight, we children walked those tracks because they provided shortcuts to a friend's house, a store, or a swimming hole. We balanced on the rails or skipped from tie to tie, avoiding the gravel packed in between. Our journeys were always limited, but the rails stretched into infinity.

We were largely a law-abiding town, but Cumberland did boast a small police force to keep it that way. One officer, on the lookout for scofflaw parking violators, tooled around town in a small one-person vehicle manufactured by the Nebraska-based Cushman Co. The vehicle, a couple of evolutionary steps up from a golf cart, lacked for speed but made up for that in cost effectiveness. Unfortunately, the Cushman comically undermined the officer's authority, puncturing the pomposity with which he carried out his duties. My friends and I snickered when he drove past, knowing that in the event of a car chase, his sputtering means of transportation would be no match for the kind of black-sedan villains Dick Tracy tracked down.

My earliest personal encounter with a Cumberland police officer came when I was about four. He arrived at our door investigating the case of a miscreant youth who, armed with a BB gun, had shot out windows in the neighborhood. A poorly informed stool pigeon had told the officer that the Blairs had a son and perhaps the officer would be wise to interrogate my mother about her boy's whereabouts at the time of the crime.

The officer loomed large in our doorway, and I peeked out from behind my mother, wondering if I was about to be hauled off to jail like those evildoers on *77 Sunset Strip*, my favorite TV detective show at the time. The officer appeared amused as my mother introduced me and assured him that I did not own a BB gun (she would not allow such a thing) nor was I permitted to roam far from her watchful eye.

The investigation evolved into a friendly chat, easing my worries of being led away in ill-fitting handcuffs. The officer noticed that I could not take my eyes off his gun, which looked so much more powerful than the cap pistols my mother did allow me to carry. He winked at me.

"You like the gun?" he asked. "When I run out of bullets, I'll come back and give it to you."

My young mind began to calculate how long it might take him to exhaust his bullet supply, and I prayed for a massive crime spree to hit Cumberland. This day was turning out pretty well after all. My name had been cleared, and I was a few *Untouchables*-style shootouts away from owning an extraordinary prize.

My father laughed when my mother and I told him of the day's adventure and the officer's carefully crafted promise to me.

"I don't think he will be running out of bullets any time soon," Dad said.

Although Cumberland's criminal element was limited, the town had its characters. One man walked the streets loudly talking to himself, as if explaining something of importance to an unseen companion. He was harmless, though, much like the character of Elwood P. Dowd in the movie *Harvey*. We ignored him and any six-foot, three-and-a-half-inch invisible rabbits tagging along at his side.

Nature on occasion took its toll. Looney Creek, a meandering small river, cut through the middle of town, its waters threatening to swell over the banks in times of heavy rain. Whenever I walked across one of the town's bridges after a torrential storm, the risen stream would roar beneath me, proclaiming its power to create havoc.

Cumberland indeed experienced a serious flood in 1957, with water pouring onto Main Street. Our town wasn't alone in its suffering. The National Weather Service reported that in late January and early February of that year, rising waters had devastated many mountain communities in Kentucky, West Virginia, Virginia, and Tennessee. Roads became impassable, some water supplies were contaminated, and many residents hastily evacuated, forced to leave behind precious belongings.

Mostly, weather proved more moderate. It rained some, it snowed some, and on summer days the sun shone brightly enough that teenagers could spread out beach towels in their backyards in hopes of improving their tans.

Then there were the liquor stores.

Cumberland was a "wet" town in an otherwise "dry" county. In fact, most of southeastern Kentucky was dry. Decades after the rest of the country determined Prohibition was a poorly thought-out idea, it was still in full force in the mountains, likely thanks to a strange alliance of religious teetotalers and whiskey smugglers. As local wags liked to put it, opposition to the legal sale of alcohol was one thing preachers and bootleggers could agree on.

For those who desired to buy their alcohol legally, Cumberland served as a tantalizing oasis in an otherwise parched region, with several liquor stores eager to meet

> **As local wags liked to put it, opposition to the legal sale of alcohol was one thing preachers and bootleggers could agree on.**

the demand. A quirk in state law gave our tiny town more than its share of such stores. Kentucky placed a limit on the number of licenses that could be issued for the sale of alcoholic beverages, but the state calculated that limit based on county population. Since Cumberland was Harlan County's only wet area, the town was awarded all of the county's licenses. Some people claimed our town had more liquor stores than churches, but I never bothered to count.

Recreation in Cumberland was limited, though we children played in our yards and, as we grew older, hiked the mountains, swam in rivers, and pedaled banana-seat bicycles from one end of town to the other. A city park, later eliminated for a road expansion, provided playground equipment and pavilions for picnics. Beyond that, the thirteen-hundred-acre Kingdom Come State Park, sitting at an elevation of twenty-seven thousand feet atop Pine Mountain along the Little Shepherd Trail, was a favorite destination for Labor Day picnics, school field trips, or impromptu family outings.

Anytime my parents said, "Let's go to Kingdom Come," I needed no coaxing. The park boasted breathtaking scenic overlooks, a cave amphitheater, and impressive rock formations. The latter included Raven's Rock, an enticing 290-foot-high rock exposure that slanted against a hillside at a forty-five-degree angle. Raven's Rock was our

Mount Everest. We watched enviously as older kids scaled the rock, disappearing from sight as they reached its peak, where, we were told, you could find the King's Chair and the Queen's Chair (additional rock formations vaguely resembling thrones) and the Devil's Bathtub (a sunken spot that collected water).

You might think that at a place called Raven's Rock you would find ravens aplenty, but you and Edgar Allan Poe would be disappointed. As a reporter for *The Courier-Journal* in Louisville noted in 1960, "Folklore has it that Raven's Rock was once the nesting place of great hordes of ravens. The name clings today although the ravens are not to be found."

Getting to Kingdom Come State Park was quite the feat in and of itself. A steep, winding, narrow road took you up the mountain to the entrance. You knew you had arrived when the road leveled and a 3.5-acre man-made lake appeared. People fished the lake for large-mouth bass, bluegill, catfish, and other fish, an activity that continues to this day.

In the early to mid-1960s, in the first few years after the park opened, people also swam in the lake. One day my family visited the park and stood near the water, admiring the beauty around us. Three young men in their late teens or early twenties were taking a dip, and as a boy who had not yet learned to swim, I envied them as they plowed through the water with strong strokes. One of them swam in our direction and waded out near us. A second one swam toward the farther shore, where he took a seat on the ground a few feet from the water.

It was nearing sunset, and my parents were planning to leave soon, when we heard a cry for help. The third swimmer had remained in the middle of the lake and was struggling to stay above water. No one acted at first. I think the swimmer's friends interpreted his urgent cries as a prankish attempt to fool them, and perhaps everyone else did as well. But then he went under and came back up gasping and thrashing.

Horrified at the realization that this was no joke, his pals plunged into the lake and swam swiftly out to him. They pulled him from the water on the shore opposite from where we stood as a pall came over the park's blissful setting. Mom and Dad led us on a short walk around the lake to where a small crowd had gathered to check on the young man's condition. He was very much alive but clearly shaken, his face ashen. He avoided making eye contact with the anxious people hovering about him, perhaps uncomfortable with the attention that near-death experiences bring. Near him I could see vomit where he had thrown up. It was a stark ending to an otherwise pleasant day.

Soon after that, "No Swimming" signs appeared at the lake. The park was taking no more chances. All of us had been given a harsh reminder that life can turn on a dime—or a missed swimming stroke.

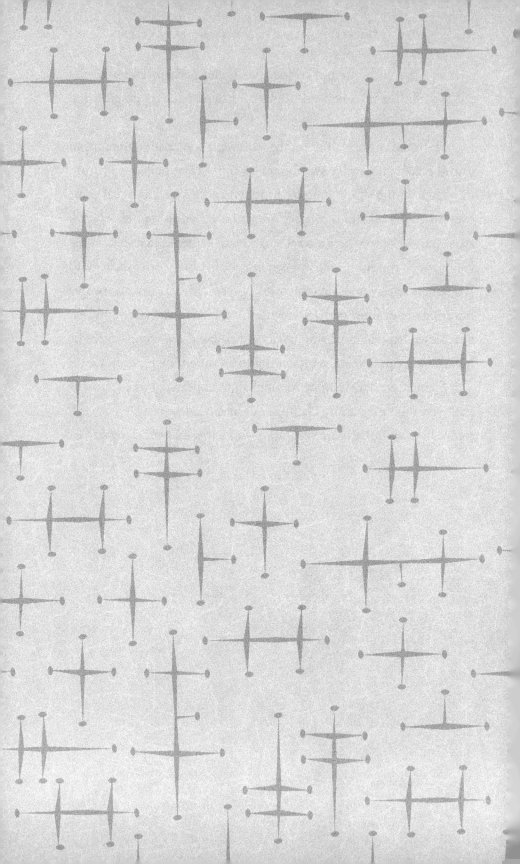

CHAPTER 5

A HOOSIER INTERLUDE

A year or so after I was born, the coal mine where my father worked announced unsettling news. Times were tough, and they were laying people off—Dad included. This was one more cruel blow for a man who, not yet forty, had had his childhood stolen by the Depression, his young adulthood stolen by a world war, and his first son's life stolen by a heart defect.

But with a wife and two children to support at that point, he had no time to rage at the universe. He needed to act quickly to find another job. The opportunity came with the help of a brother-in-law who worked for a construction company in Shelbyville, Indiana, and arranged for the company to hire Dad.

Off we went to Shelbyville, a town that at least had a Kentucky connection, having been named for Kentucky's first governor, Isaac Shelby. About fourteen thousand people lived in Shelbyville, making it more than three times the size of Cumberland. I have no memory of our time there, but I was told we lived in an apartment where the landlady displayed no patience for noisy children and developed an instant dislike for Shelia and me, not in the least bewitched by our innate cuteness.

I was never clear on the events that led to Dad's sudden unemployment, but research provided a potential clue. In 1959, a four-month steelworkers' strike did more than shut down steel mills. Workers in other industries felt the effects as well, including thousands of coal miners whose livelihood was snatched away, seeing as the shuttered steel mills needed no coal to fire idle blast furnaces. At least half a million workers nationwide experienced some effect directly or indirectly from the strike, according to a 1960 report by the US Department of Labor.

The situation became so dire that President Eisenhower intervened, using a provision of the Taft-Hartley Act to order the steelworkers back to work. Initially, Eisenhower's order met with one big collective steelworker shrug. They weren't soldiers, and this wasn't Normandy. The United Steelworkers of America decided to confront Eisenhower and take the case to court, intent on getting the Taft-Hartley Act declared unconstitutional. That didn't happen. The US Supreme Court sided with the president, and after 116 days, the strike ended. The chastened steelworkers returned to work, and other people did, too.

Dad learned he could reclaim his coal-mining job, which meant he faced a decision: stay in Indiana and stick with the construction job or uproot his family for the second time in a few short months and return home to Kentucky. One factor made selecting his course of action easier. The steel strike, the mine layoff, and the Indiana job opportunity all happened so quickly that Mom and Dad had never gotten all their possessions moved to Shelbyville. Not only were their hearts in Kentucky, but so were many of their belongings, likely in the safekeeping of a friend or relative.

Dad later told me that if everything they owned had been moved, he would have stayed in Shelbyville, and our lives would have taken a completely different trajectory. As it was, we bid farewell to our brief life as Hoosiers and headed back to the mountains.

I imagine our poor put-upon landlady sang silent praises to President Eisenhower and the Taft-Hartley Act as the four of us sped away.

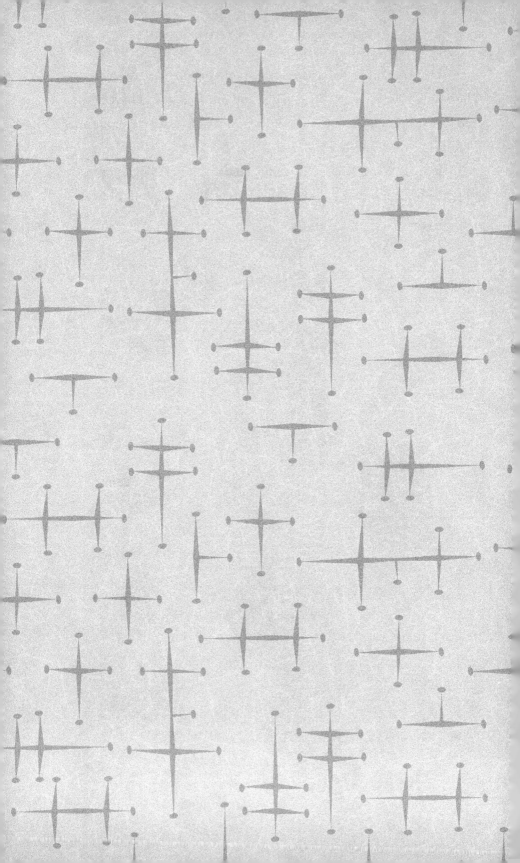

CHAPTER 6

THE HOUSES THAT BUILT ME

In 2010, country singer Miranda Lambert released a hit song titled *The House That Built Me*, which tells of a woman returning to her childhood home and trying to recapture cherished memories, such as practicing guitar in her bedroom and burying a beloved dog under an oak tree in the yard.

In my case, not one but three houses built me. I think of them this way: the Hole, Jackson Hill, and School Road.

My earliest memories involve living in what we referred to as the Hole, although of course it was not an actual hole. We were not a family of rabbits, after all. To get to the Hole, you drove up the road on Indian Hill, but before reaching the top you would see another road that veered off to the left, dipping down into a small area tucked tightly into the hill. This was the Hole.

Three small houses sat in the Hole. The first was ours, or at least we rented it. Next door lived Bill and Anna Gay Chavies, parents to a son and daughter much older than us and later to twin daughters slightly younger. Living in the third house was the Polis family, which included a son named Tommy who was Shelia's age. Due to the proximity of our houses and a lack of other children in the Hole, Tommy became our closest friend. We played games, shared bags of potato chips, and luxuriated in the blissful childhood knowledge that adults would take care of any difficulties that arose while we tended to the idle hours that filled our days. Then one day we received troubling news.

"We're moving," Tommy told us, giving Shelia and me an early lesson in the ways in which life can be disrupted by events beyond our control.

We watched forlornly as Tommy's family vacated the Hole. Fortunately, their house didn't remain empty for long. A family with a girl our age took up residence there, providing us a replacement playmate.

The house we rented in the Hole was tiny and barely functional for what eventually, with the birth of Ricky in 1960, would be a family of five. The front door opened into a cramped living room furnished with a couch, a chair, and a black-and-white TV. In one corner stood a coal stove that provided heat. There were two bedrooms and one bathroom, which had a shower stall but no bathtub, so Mom bathed us in a washtub. The kitchen also functioned as the dining room and infirmary, where Mom served us fried chicken, banana pudding, and other savory delights as well as ministered to our bee stings, cuts, and hurt feelings. In the back of the house stood a coal shed that backed up against the hill. We had no backyard, but we did have a side yard where Dad erected a swing set to keep us occupied.

The house had a small front porch where Mom could sit and keep an eye on us as we played. One day she bolted up horrified when a rattlesnake slithered through the grass right past me as I cavorted about the yard. She pulled me onto the porch and watched uneasily as the snake crossed the road and disappeared into the weeds. Dad was at work, so Mom alerted Mr. Chavies to see if he could perhaps kill the intruder that was as much a threat to his family as ours. But after a cautious search, our neighbor found no sign of the snake. Instead of feeling relief, I now eyed those weeds warily.

During this time, I owned a red pedal car that became involved in a notorious one-car crash. One day, Shelia, the new neighborhood girl, and I decided it would be a marvelous idea to push the pedal car to the top of the hill and coast down triumphantly to our house. We took along Ricky, who was perhaps two. If my mother ever proclaimed, "I can't look away from you kids for one second," she was correct.

We sat Ricky on the tiny car's hood. I took the driver's seat, and Shelia and the other girl squeezed in as best they could, seeing as pedal cars are not well designed for excess passengers. We began our descent with joyful laughter that quickly evolved into shrieks of terror. We had not counted on how gravity, the steepness of the hill, and the pedal car's lack of brakes would combine to give us a ride worthy of an amusement park.

The road leveled off in front of our house, but it also curved to the left. In a valiant effort to keep the speeding pedal car on the road, I turned the steering wheel sharply—too sharply. The pedal car left the road, plunging into the weeds and down a small incline, where it came to an unceremonious halt. Shelia, the other girl, and I abandoned Ricky and scurried out of the weeds and across the road, screaming all the way. My mother, alarmed by the cries of three distressed youngsters, emerged from the house to see her youngest child still sitting quietly atop the pedal car's hood and surrounded by the same weeds she once watched a rattlesnake slither into.

She plunged into the weeds and down the short slope to retrieve Ricky, but she left the pedal car where it rested. As the vehicle's owner,

I was outraged by this injustice and stared despondently at my now unreachable property. Technically, it was reachable, but Mom was not about to risk the wrath of snakes for the sake of a pedal car, and neither was I. Later, Mr. Chavies nonchalantly pulled the car from nature's treacherous hold and brought it back to my grateful arms.

The doomed pedal-car excursion was perhaps the last significant event we experienced in the Hole. In 1963 we moved to 409 Cornett Street, atop what was referred to as Jackson Hill. The two-story house we rented there was unusual in that both stories were at ground level. How is that possible? The house had been built into the side of a hill. You entered the front door at the top of the hill. You descended the stairs and exited the back door farther down the hill.

This house was much larger than the one in the Hole, with three or four bedrooms and even a drafty playroom, where we kept a disorganized collection of excess toys. Like the house in the Hole, our Jackson Hill abode was heated by a coal stove, although inadequately. Staying warm on winter nights required extra quilts and excessive praying.

"Get under the covers and stay still. You'll warm up," Mom insisted, though I harbored doubts.

At least this time my parents didn't need to go outside to a shed to retrieve the fuel for the stove. The man who delivered coal dumped our supply down a chute next to the house, and my parents could access that chute through a door at the bottom of the stairs.

The property also came with a hillside garden that my mother wanted to put to immediate use, so my parents hired a man to plow it. He appeared on a sunny morning, wearing a wide-brimmed hat and leading a mule. The man harnessed the mule to the plow, and the two of them plodded back and forth, breaking up the soil to create the furrows where Mom would cultivate her tomatoes, green beans, and potatoes. I watched in awe as the man and the animal went about their work. For one brief moment on a glorious Kentucky morning, plowing a garden appeared to be the greatest achievement anyone could aspire to, and I imagined myself on some far-off day with my own mule and my own garden to tackle.

> For one brief moment on a glorious Kentucky morning, plowing a garden appeared to be the greatest achievement anyone could aspire to.

My mule never materialized, but in a few short years Mom put me to work pulling weeds, planting potatoes, and hoeing. I grumbled and protested every step of the way.

At the bottom of our backyard hill lay the equivalent of a wonderland playground, at least for a kid in a neighborhood that was part subdivision, part rural farm community. A barn stood next to a pasture where a lone cow grazed. In the middle of the pasture was a covered pig pen that, no doubt, had once served as home to a hog that possibly met an untimely end and became someone's Christmas feast. Now the pen stood empty and worth investigating. One day when I was six or seven, I was playing in the pasture and crawled through an opening in the pig pen. Almost instantly I felt a painful sting. I jumped back and felt more stings.

I had disturbed a wasp nest. The wasps were not amused. They swarmed me as I raced frantically across the pasture, screaming for help as each dive bomber inflicted another blow. Mom rushed out of the house, hurried down the hill, assessed the situation, grabbed me, and scurried back to the house for safety. There she tended to my wounds while I sniffled in despair, both from the pain caused by the wasp's venom and because my adventure had ended so abruptly and violently. Clearly, the pasture came with dangers, and exploring its environs was fraught with peril.

I did not learn my lesson.

On a spring day in 1966 I ventured into the barn, my eight-year-old imagination transforming the structure into Wayne Manor, home of Batman, who at the time was featured on my favorite TV series. That a barn in no way resembles a millionaire's mansion did not deter me. The barn loft could serve as Wayne Manor itself. The barn's floor, which was just earth, would be the Bat Cave. Proud of my ingenuity, I climbed up to Wayne Manor, pondering which villain—the Joker, the Riddler, the Penguin, Catwoman—would create havoc and require me to transform into the Caped Crusader.

On the TV show, Batman and Robin used Bat Poles hidden behind a bookcase to slide down to the Bat Cave, mysteriously changing from street clothes into crime-fighting costumes by the time they reached bottom. The barn had no Bat Pole, so I decided to approximate my heroes' descent by hanging over the edge of the loft and dropping. It was a poor substitute, but you worked with what you had. Before I could properly position myself, I lost my grip and fell. A sharp pain shot through my left knee the moment I landed.

Crying in agony, I exited the barn. My shrieks attracted the attention of two older boys who lived on a hill on the opposite side of the barn. Alarmed, they descended a hillside flight of steps to investigate.

One boy eyed the source of my pain with concern.

"Pull up your pants leg," he said, pointing to my left leg.

Sobbing, I complied. I sobbed even more when I saw blood pouring from a deep and wide gash in my knee. The other boy had seen blood on my pants that I'd failed to notice.

"Where's your mom?" he asked, puzzled that she hadn't appeared immediately when I began wailing.

"Mrs. Dixon's house," I managed to say through gasps of pain and fright.

Mrs. Dixon lived a few houses farther down Jackson Hill. One boy hustled off to find Mom while the other helped me up the hill to our house.

This was the day I learned what stitches are. My knee required nine of them, along with a tightly wound bandage that kept my left leg immobile. It remained that way for the next few weeks, and people jokingly dubbed me "Chester" after a limping character in the popular TV show *Gunsmoke.* So, at least the stitches provided some amusement. I steered clear of the barn loft after that, though.

In the summer of 1967, it came time to move again because my parents decided to give up the renters' life and finally, in their forties, become homeowners. They bought a small house that sat directly across the street from Cumberland Elementary School at 713 School Road.

I loved our new house, although in retrospect, with two bedrooms and one bathroom, it did not truly meet the needs of a family of five. The location gave us a short walk to school, though, and the large backyard provided a generous playground for Shelia, Ricky, and me. The house also came with a detached garage that, in addition to providing shelter for our 1964 Chevrolet Malibu, could be used for storage.

The house did not remain small—or at least not as small. My parents hired a man to build a third bedroom.

Our yard backed up to a tiny cemetery, and a wire fence was all that separated us from headstones jutting from the Kentucky soil. I could stand at the fence and read the names of the dead. Surprisingly, despite my extraordinary imagination for the supernatural, this proximity to the hereafter did not haunt my dreams or cause me uneasiness.

Mom, ever the gardener, claimed the back portion of the yard as her own, anyway, and planted vegetables that she would then can and keep in our basement, occasionally sending me down to retrieve green beans or other potential side dishes as she prepared supper.

Even with the garden and a clothesline stealing a portion of the yard, we still had ample room for football, kickball, tag, and other activities. Dad bemoaned how our spirited outdoor games tore up the grass in his lovely backyard. Mom chided him.

"One day," she said, "you are going to look out the window and wish they were out there tearing up the yard."

CHAPTER 7

SIXTEEN TONS— AND THEN SOME

My hometown's economy depended largely on one industry—coal mining.

Each day, men in the town (and by the late 1970s, some women) arrived at one of the area's many mines and donned hard-toed boots as well as a hard hat that was topped off by a removable light. A cord from the light ran down to a large battery attached to a thick belt around the waist. A small piece of metal with an engraved number was bolted to the belt. That number served as backup identification in case a fatal explosion left a miner's features damaged beyond recognition.

> While miners were cognizant of the job's dangers and took proper precautions, they did not ponder mortality all that much on a day-to-day basis.

That might sound morbid, but while miners were cognizant of the job's dangers and took proper precautions, they did not ponder mortality all that much on a day-to-day basis as they prepared to earn their wages. After exchanging a few jokes and pleasantries, they would board a mantrip, a low-slung vehicle that transported them into the mine. The miners rode the mantrip lying on their backs with their lights turned off. They stared quietly into darkness or briefly dozed off as the mantrip delivered them to their underground stop for the day.

Then they would begin their jobs: roof bolter, continuous-mine operator, shuttle-car driver, general inside labor. Pay was determined by both the union contract and a particular job's hazards. Roof bolters earned the most because they took the greatest risk. It was their job to venture into a recently mined-out tunnel where nothing supported the mine roof. They installed the bolts that would hold the top firm so the other miners could come in with some, but not complete, confidence.

Even a bolted roof had its hazards. Large pieces of rock could break free, crushing an unsuspecting miner. The miners kept a close lookout for loose top and used a crowbar to pull down anything that appeared unstable.

Mines often had low top, which meant headroom did not exist. Miners walked and worked bent over, careful to avoid scraping their backs on the ends of the roof bolts protruding from the top. It was a luxury to stand straight.

In his 1937 book *The Road to Wigan Pier*, George Orwell painted a grim picture of working conditions inside a coal mine. "Most of the things one imagines in hell are there—heat, noise, confusion, darkness, foul air, and, above all, unbearably cramped space," Orwell wrote. "Everything except the fire, for there is no fire down there except the feeble beams of Davy lamps and electric torches which scarcely penetrate the clouds of coal dust."

Orwell's description was based on time spent visiting a mine in the north of England in the 1930s, not a southeastern Kentucky mine in the 1960s and 1970s, where miners kept those clouds of coal dust to a minimum by coating the mine walls with pulverized limestone. But the overall image holds up, and Orwell, whose life's work involved crafting words while seated at a typewriter, came away with a healthy respect for miners. He imagined that, if necessary, he could manage life as a "tolerable road-sweeper or an inefficient gardener or even a tenth-rate farm hand. But by no conceivable amount of effort or training could I become a coal miner," Orwell wrote. "The work would kill me in a few weeks."

Beyond the risk mining itself created, in the early twentieth century tensions in Harlan County grew between miners and the mining companies, which often controlled every aspect of miners' lives. The situation was perhaps best captured by the 1946 song *Sixteen Tons*, written by Merle Travis and made into a hit by singer Tennessee Ernie Ford. The song described a miner's situation as so dire that his debt included owing the company store his very soul.

That was an exaggeration—but not by much. Miners often owed their advance wages to the company store, and getting out from underneath that debt was nearly impossible. By the 1930s, with the Great Depression in full swing and many Harlan County miners unemployed or taking pay cuts, animosity between mine operators and miners escalated into violence. Unions sought to make inroads, and mine operators fiercely fought that effort. The result was gunshots, bombings, murders, and, as the subtitle of one book from the era put it, "terrorism in the Kentucky coal fields." The governor ordered the Kentucky National Guard into the county on more than one occasion to try to quell the violence.

As a result, Harlan County attracted national attention. *New York Times* headlines included, "Kentucky Troops Mobilize in Harlan" and "Bomb in Auto Kills Kentucky Official." The latter referred to the 1935 murder of County Attorney Elmon Middleton.

Theodore Dreiser, author of such novels as *Sister Carrie* and *An American Tragedy*, led a journalistic effort to expose how coal operators and local officials treated Harlan County miners. That effort resulted in a 1932 book titled *Harlan Miners Speak: Report on Terrorism in the Kentucky Coal Fields*. In addition to Dreiser, the book's twelve contributing writers included John Dos Passos and Sherwood Anderson.

Here's an excerpt from how Anderson, best known for his book *Winesburg, Ohio*, described the situation in my home county:

The eyes of the whole country had become focused on that little spot. It had become a little ugly running sore, workers being beaten, women thrown into jail, American citizens being terrorized, newspaper men trying to investigate, being shot and terrorized. When you have got a disease inside the body it has a nasty little trick of breaking out in little sores of that sort.

Dreiser's National Committee for the Defense of Political Prisoners took testimony from miners, their wives, journalists, and others in the community. When Dreiser asked a woman what the members of one union wanted, she replied, "They are asking for a little more bread and meat for the starving people, better homes to live in and Harlan County a fit place to live in, and coal miners regarded as more than as jack rabbits to be shot at."

Harlan County's violent coal strikes seemed like ancient history to me because by the time I arrived on the scene twenty-six years after Dreiser's report, the situation had changed drastically. The United Mine Workers of America was firmly entrenched, miners and their families shopped where they pleased, and strikes that happened whenever the union contract expired tended to progress peacefully.

But in 1973 things began to heat up again at the Brookside Mine near Evarts. Miners there went on strike against the Eastover Mining Co., a subsidiary of Duke Power. Those miners wanted to join the United Mine Workers like their brethren elsewhere in the county, putting an end to their meager wages and the squalid conditions in which they and their families lived. Their reality was much different from the one I experienced in the same county in the same time period with a father in the same vocation.

As a teenager, I was somewhat aware of what was happening at Brookside, and once when the Cumberland High School football team scheduled a preseason scrimmage with Evarts High School, our bus passed by the pickets. Largely, though, this was an out-of-sight, out-of-mind strike for those of us in Cumberland, which was nearly twenty miles away.

For the rest of the country, it was a replay of early-twentieth-century mountain violence. The strike became immortalized in the 1976 Academy Award–winning documentary *Harlan County, USA*, directed by Barbara Kopple. The thirteen-month Brookside Mine strike ended in August 1974, two days after a twenty-two-year-old miner named Lawrence Jones died in a shootout with a mine foreman.

Barbara Kopple was still a few months away from releasing *Harlan County, USA* when the nation's eyes once again turned to the coal fields of southeastern Kentucky. On March 9, 1976, just before noon, an explosion ripped through the Scotia Mine in Letcher County, about fourteen miles northeast of Cumberland, killing fifteen miners. Later, it was determined that faulty equipment ignited methane in the poorly ventilated mine. Those of us in Cumberland couldn't ignore this event, because some of those miners lived in our community.

A couple of days after the Scotia Mine accident, I went through my usual before-school routine. I arose early and turned on the radio, which was always tuned to WCPM, Cumberland's lone radio station. Typically, I listened as the DJ played the top hits of the day, such as *Love Rollercoaster*, by the Ohio Players, or *50 Ways to Leave Your Lover*, by Paul Simon.

But this morning, not surprisingly, the voice from the radio was talking about Scotia, which continued to cast a somber haze over the region. Still, as I listened, it struck me that something didn't seem quite right. Finally, it became clear why. The radio announcer was not talking about the accident from two days ago. There had been a second explosion at the mine, killing eleven miners and mine inspectors who were investigating the cause of the first tragedy.

As if the deaths of those eleven men weren't heart wrenching enough, it was now considered too dangerous to attempt any more recovery missions—at least right away. Their bodies would remain entombed in the mine for 253 days. Finally, in November, by which time I had started my freshman year at Morehead State University, the bodies were retrieved so their families could bury them.

The only positive note from this mournful moment in the region's history is that the Scotia Mine disaster led Congress to pass the Federal Mine Safety and Health Act of 1977. But those added protections for miners came much too late for Scotia's twenty-six victims.

CHAPTER 8

DAD GOES TO WAR

World War II loomed large over childhood in the 1960s. Nearly every war game played out in our backyards involved fending off Germans. We watched dramatic TV series set during the war such as *Combat, The Rat Patrol, Garrison's Gorillas,* and *Twelve O'Clock High.* We read comic books such as *Sgt. Fury and His Howling Commandos* and *Our Army at War featuring Sgt. Rock.* On the living room floor we staged elaborate battles with plastic toy soldiers who defended the world from Hitler's treachery.

Many of us, myself included, had fathers who, two decades earlier, had fought in that war.

In our house hung a photo from my father's army days. Written at the bottom of the photo were the words *Company L, 19th Infantry, Schofield Barracks, Hawaii, June 1941.* In the photo, Dad was the second soldier from the right in the second row from the top.

How he ended up in that photo is a story that's likely typical of many of the men of Company L.

The world faced difficult times in the late 1930s. The Great Depression lingered, and Dad struggled to find reliable employment. Finally, at age twenty and with job opportunities scarce, he decided the army could provide the regular paycheck he so desperately needed. Not that it would be an extraordinary amount. The peacetime army paid twenty-one dollars a month, according to *Pearl Harbor Ghosts: The Legacy of December 7, 1941*, by Thurston Clarke. Regardless, Dad enlisted and was inducted on July 5, 1940, in Richmond, Virginia. Although the United States was not at war yet, Germany was already causing problems across Europe, and five days later the Battle of Britain would begin.

Once Dad became a soldier, he was not destined to stay on the mainland for long. Two months after his enlistment, he shipped out for Hawaii, arriving in Oahu on September 26, 1940, where he reported for duty at Schofield Barracks.

Moving in such a short period of time from the back hills of Kentucky to the tropics of Hawaii must have been quite the culture shock. But in a sense Dad had traded one geographically secluded place for another, and Hawaii wasn't a paradise for the 1940s infantry in the same way it is for tourists today. Clarke wrote in *Pearl Harbor Ghosts* that "many servicemen loathed the Islands. Some had not seen their families for almost two years, and they pursued the lonely-man pastimes of beer drinking and card playing, fighting with local youths they called 'gooks,' and sitting on shoreline rocks, heads in hands, staring toward San Francisco. Their suicide rate was higher than on mainland bases, and in October 1941, one despondent soldier the

Hawaii wasn't a paradise for the 1940s infantry in the same way it is for tourists today.

newspapers called a 'human bomb' threw himself from the roof of the University Cinema onto the orchestra seats.'"

The army was busy making changes in Hawaii as the summer of 1941 drew to an end. From August to September, the Hawaiian Division was reorganized into two divisions—the Twenty-Fourth and the Twenty-Fifth. As a result, the Nineteenth Infantry that Dad belonged to became part of the Twenty-Fourth Infantry Division.

On the fateful morning of December 7, 1941, Dad was assigned guard duty, though I'm not certain whether he was at Schofield Barracks' main gate, somewhere else on the base, or perhaps at another location on the island that the army felt warranted a soldier's presence. That he was both awake and on duty at that early hour made him unusual among the men of the Twenty-Fourth and Twenty-Fifth Divisions. In his book *Day of Infamy*, Walter Lord wrote that many Schofield soldiers "were on weekend pass to Honolulu; others had straggled home in the early hours and were dead to the world." Dad was neither on a weekend pass nor sleeping off a night of revelry on what, by all accounts, started off as a serene morning. Somewhere around 7:55 a.m. he heard the hum of airplanes and looked up to see a fleet of planes in the distance. He had no reason to count, but they numbered 353.

Initially, Dad paid them little mind. He knew they didn't belong to the army, but the navy also had planes, and he assumed these might be navy pilots on maneuvers. An explosion from the direction of the harbor told him otherwise. In an instant, the island was under attack. Smoke billowed from Pearl Harbor as the ships there were bombed and torpedoed. At Hickam Field next to Pearl Harbor, about twenty-five Japanese dive bombers dropped their bombs on army planes that were neatly lined up and provided easy targets. The Japanese also attacked Wheeler Field next to Schofield, similarly taking out aircraft.

Once they finished at Wheeler, the Japanese pilots turned their attention to Schofield Barracks, strafing the quadrangles and buildings. Soldiers at Schofield responded as best they could, firing machine guns, Springfield rifles, and pistols at the swooping Japanese planes. Here's how one soldier quoted in Thurston Clarke's book described the scene and the mood: "We wore World War I pie-plate helmets, were lightly armed, and our average age was nineteen. We all thought we were going to die."

Dad spoke little about his actions after the attack began, other than to say, "I guess I had enough sense to shoot my gun." Years later, he was still haunted by the memory of seeing "the dead bodies of all those eighteen-year-old boys," likely a reference to sailors since Schofield did not suffer the brunt of the attack the way the navy's fleet in Pearl Harbor did. Dad's Twenty-Fourth Infantry Division saw nine men wounded and one killed, while two soldiers with the Twenty-Fifth Infantry Division were killed and seventeen wounded, according to the Twenty-Fifth Infantry Division Association's website. Corporal Theodore J. Lewis earned the unenviable distinction of being the first member of the Twenty-Fourth Infantry Division to be killed in action in World War II.

The attack lasted one hour and fifteen minutes. As the Japanese planes retreated, their work done, no one on the island thought it was over. Military commanders assumed the air attack was the first wave, and they anticipated Japanese ships carrying an invasion force would soon arrive to take control of the island and make prisoners of everyone on it.

The soldiers of Schofield Barracks established positions all around the island to await that invasion, constructing pillboxes and stringing barbed wire along the beaches. Dad's Twenty-Fourth Infantry Division was assigned the task of defending northern Oahu while the Twenty-

Fifth took care of the island's southern half. Throughout the night of December 7 and into the morning of December 8, as President Roosevelt gave his "infamy" speech to Congress nearly five thousand miles away, the soldiers eyed the darkness over the Pacific and braced themselves for a battle that never came. The island, under martial law by now, remained jittery until June 1942, when an American victory at the Battle of Midway lessened the likelihood that my father would need to help defend Oahu from a second Japanese attack.

Still, Dad remained in Hawaii for another year after Midway, but by September 1943, he and the rest of the Twenty-Fourth Infantry Division had relocated to Camp Caves, a training facility in Australia, where they prepared for battle against the Japanese in Dutch New Guinea.

Dad considered Australia the most beautiful place he visited during his army days, with his memories of Hawaii's tropical splendor perhaps tainted by the horrors of December 7, 1941. "If I could go back and visit one place," he said, "it would be Australia."

But this interlude in the Land Down Under lasted only a few short months.

In January 1944, Dad moved with the division to Goodenough Island in the Solomon Sea. The Australian military had seized the island from a Japanese occupying force in October 1942, and the Allies had maintained possession of it since then, building airstrips and other facilities in anticipation of the battles to come. Goodenough Island, which lies east of the mainland of New Guinea, would serve as the staging area for the Hollandia-Tanahmerah campaign.

Up until this point, the Twenty-Fourth Division's combat experience was limited to its engagement with those Japanese planes during the attack on Pearl Harbor. Now, more than two years after the United States' entry into the war, Dad prepared for his first real taste of infantry-style combat. What followed—the Battle of Hollandia that lasted from April 22 to June 6, 1944, and took the lives of more than 150 Americans and 3,300 Japanese—was an experience he never talked about with any depth or detail.

The Twenty-Fourth Division was given its mission, a plan with the less-than-reassuring name Operation Reckless. The division would head for Tanahmerah Bay at Hollandia, a port on the northern coast of New Guinea. Simultaneously, the Forty-First Division would land at Humboldt Bay, twenty-five miles to the east. The two divisions' initial goal was to take control of three Japanese airfields that, by then, would have already been crippled by Allied bombing. They then would wrest control of New Guinea from any remaining Japanese troops, supplying a victory key to General Douglas MacArthur's plan to win the war in the Pacific.

Operation Reckless was a massive operation and my father one small player. In all, the mission involved 37,527 combat troops and 18,184 service and support troops, "all of whom would be both transported to the landing sites and protected by more than 200 naval vessels," author James P. Duffy wrote in his book *War at the End of the World*.

The Twenty-Fourth and Forty-First Divisions began their assault on the beaches at dawn on April 22 after a naval bombardment helped soften Japanese defenses. American and Australian pilots added an air attack. Upon arrival, my father would have seen the Cyclops Mountains rising seven thousand feet in the distance and would have been greeted by sporadic small arms and machine gun fire that the overwhelming American forces quickly and forcibly put an end to.

In addition to the Japanese, an extraordinarily difficult terrain greeted the soldiers. A swamp lay not far from the shoreline, and there was limited area to bring vehicles ashore. As a result, some of the lagging transports were redirected and took the remaining Twenty-Fourth Division troops instead to Humboldt Bay, where the geography was more hospitable.

Over the coming days, Dad and the Twenty-Fourth Division moved inland. They encountered some Japanese resistance, and technically the Battle of Hollandia would not be considered over until June 6. But the Japanese on the island were largely overmatched, and Operation Reckless became a great success for the Allies.

In many ways, the New Guinea terrain proved a greater foe for the Americans than the Japanese. In his book *MacArthur's Jungle War: The 1944 New Guinea Campaign*, historian Stephen R. Taaffe wrote that one person called the island "a military nightmare":

"A nightmare indeed, and in more than one way," Taaffe wrote. "Behind New Guinea's beautiful green-carpeted mountains, placid coastline, and bright-blue ocean lurked countless hazards that threatened a GI's life and limb as much as Japanese bullets, which were numerous enough."

Those hazards included jagged, impassable mountains, the swamp along the coast, and a jungle full of razor-sharp kunai grass. Mosquitoes swarmed about. Scorpions provided a real threat. And leeches could attach themselves to unwitting soldiers. The Americans were at risk of contracting malaria, dengue fever, blackwater fever, amebic and bacillary dysentery, tropical ulcers, and other diseases.

Wrote Taaffe, "Mother Nature took her toll in other ways as well, mostly, but not exclusively, through continental torrential downpours that rotted everything from clothes to skin and rusted guns and other implements of war."

On July 12, 1944, one month after the completion of Operation Reckless, the army shipped Dad back to the United States, and he arrived on the mainland on August 1. His discharge papers simply supply these dates as part of a record of his movements. They fail to explain why he left combat at this juncture with the war still raging. But for seven months, as the Twenty-Fourth Division moved on to fight in the Philippines, he was back on American soil, taking time to travel to Kentucky during this respite from the conflict overseas. On August 17, 1944, a society-page item appeared in *The Mountain Eagle*, a weekly newspaper in Whitesburg, Kentucky, reporting that Dad had visited an aunt in Letcher County the previous weekend.

The army still needed him on the front lines, though. The infantry suffered too many casualties at the Normandy invasion and constantly was in dire need of reinforcements in Europe. Dad's engagement with the Japanese was over. His fight against the Germans was about to begin.

On March 8, 1945, he shipped out for the European theater, arriving in France ten days later, now attached to Company G in the Third Infantry Division. He was just in time to join the division as it advanced in heavy combat against the German defenses in Northern France and crossed the Rhine River into Germany on March 26.

Dad had an advantage over most of the other replacements who arrived in Europe in the period after D-Day from June 1944 through the war's end. Many had been rushed into battle with minimal training. Author Stephen E. Ambrose wrote in his book *Citizen Soldiers* that in some cases they had been on the rifle range only once and had zero experience in throwing a grenade or firing a machine gun or bazooka, Dad's least favorite task.

"The replacements paid the cost," Ambrose wrote. "Often more than half became casualties within the first three days on the line. The odds were against a replacement's surviving long enough to gain recognition and experience." One serviceman described them as "scared, shy eager youngsters" who "usually died in heaps" in the first battle.

In contrast to those green recruits, Dad had been in the army nearly five years and had experienced combat, although fighting the Japanese in a jungle wasn't quite the same as fighting Germans in the European countryside and villages. Still, he was a grizzled twenty-five-year-old veteran, not an eighteen-year-old wide-eyed draftee, and that perhaps gave him an edge when it came to survival.

He said the fighting was definitely different. The Japanese approach to combat had unnerved him. In *MacArthur's Jungle War*, Taaffe described it this way: "The Japanese saw surrender as dishonorable, and they frequently fought to the last man when most other soldiers would have given up." Dad compared the two campaigns in different parts of the world in a more personal way: "The Germans seemed to be as scared as you were. The Japanese didn't seem scared at all." Likely, this was not true, but clearly there was a greater cultural divide between the Americans and the Japanese than between the Americans and the Germans.

Regardless, either campaign could produce callous indifference to the lives of fellow humans.

One day in France or Germany, possibly after a firefight that Dad and the other Americans won decisively, a German soldier realized the folly of continuing to fight and surrendered. He dropped his weapon, raised his hands, and stumbled down a hillside in the direction of his captors, placing himself at their mercy. A soldier standing near my father raised his weapon and fired, killing the unarmed German. Dad flushed with anger at this brutal and unnecessary act, and it was all he could do to refrain from turning his own weapon on his fellow soldier.

When Dad told me this story, three decades after the fact, it was obvious the cruelty of that moment still haunted him.

When Dad told me this story, three decades after the fact, it was obvious the cruelty of that moment still haunted him. Sadly, what he witnessed was not as much of an anomaly as you might hope. In *Citizen Soldiers*, Ambrose wrote that about one-third of the more than one thousand combat veterans he interviewed "related incidents in which they saw other GIs shooting unarmed German prisoners who had their hands up." The 1998 movie *Saving Private Ryan*, for which Ambrose served as a consultant, chillingly recreates such a moment in an early scene. The first time I saw the movie, I instantly thought of my father and his experience.

Thankfully, Dad's time in the European theater would be a short one. With Soviet forces moving in on Berlin, Adolf Hitler committed suicide on April 30, 1945. A week later, on May 7, Germany surrendered.

Deciding Dad's services were no longer needed, and perhaps determining that he had done enough by fighting in both the Pacific and European theaters, the army sent him back to the United States in June, and he arrived stateside on June 28. He would never leave the United States again.

The army honorably discharged Dad on July 3, 1945, at Camp Atterbury, Indiana, in time for him to celebrate Independence Day as a civilian for the first time in five years. A month later, the United States dropped atomic bombs on the Japanese cities of Hiroshima and Nagasaki, leading to Japan's surrender and the end of the war.

Sometime in the late 1970s, Dad and I watched a news report about Vietnam War veterans and their return to civilian life. Someone in the report complained about their poor reception, so different from World War II veterans who were "greeted with parades."

"What parade?" Dad asked. "They gave me my mustering-out pay, I got on a bus, and I went home, unemployed."

CHAPTER 9

RODNEY

Rodney's picture always held a place of honor in our home.

It was a simple enough picture, a black-and-white studio shot of a young boy with big teeth that grinned mightily and squinting eyes that danced mischievously.

But if a photograph can symbolize anything, this one symbolized both life's joy and its frailty.

Rodney was my older brother. And when he was nine years old—not so long after the picture was taken—he died, finally overcome by a heart that had been bad since his birth.

His death happened in 1957, the year before I was born. I never knew him, except through his picture, his grave, and the stories my parents and other relatives told.

The stories were many. How Rodney loved to watch *Howdy Doody* and *Circus Boy* on TV. How he was intelligent enough to skip a grade in school.

And how he got a bicycle when he was about eight years old at a time when his heart was really starting to turn on him. Try as he might, he couldn't summon the strength to pedal it. So, my father sat Rodney on the bicycle and pushed him around the yard the way one might a toddler.

Sometimes when I stared at Rodney's picture, I would try to bring him to life in my mind. For in truth, I longed for this big brother, and I mourned him without having known him.

For me the picture provided more solace than did his grave, which we visited each Memorial Day. The cemetery sat on a hill. To get there we crossed a swinging bridge and then walked a small path.

It was a nice outing, almost like a picnic, only without food. But the grave was just a patch of earth marked by a headstone. I could find no clue to Rodney there the way I could by studying his grin and trying to read his eyes to see if they held secrets his little brother should know.

If the secrets existed, I never unlocked them, and in the end there was only this, the final story.

Rodney's heart got worse. The doctor told my parents they had a decision to make. They could do nothing, and Rodney would live perhaps one more year.

Or they could let the doctor operate. If the operation was a success, Rodney might lead a long life. If it was unsuccessful, he could die on the operating table.

The last time my parents saw Rodney alive, he was being rolled into the operating room. He was smiling at them.

CHAPTER 10

THE ALLIGATOR NEXT DOOR

One summer our neighbors took a trip to Florida and returned with impressive tans, numerous vacation photos, and one certifiably and authentically real baby alligator—not some rubber-toy substitute.

This turn of events piqued my small-boy curiosity as I peered through the wire fence separating our yards to get a good look at the tiny habitat the neighbors had created for this exotic creature. *Mutual of Omaha's Wild Kingdom* had plopped down practically at my door. My parents likely fretted that baby alligators grow into adult alligators, but I harbored no such worries. I envied the girl next door who owned a pet like no other in all of Cumberland.

These days, Florida tourists who are heedless of the dangers can't simply walk up to a souvenir stand and purchase baby alligators. The state has strict laws about messing around with its gators. Even feeding them in the wild can land you in trouble, because an alligator fed by humans comes to associate people with food and—well, as you can imagine, no good comes of that.

But the Sunshine State didn't always keep such a tight rein on human interaction with the reptiles. Up until the late 1960s, baby-alligator commerce was a real thing, coming to a halt in 1967 only after alligators were listed as an endangered species, according to the Florida Memory website operated by the State Library and Archives of Florida. In case there are doubters, Florida Memory includes a 1962 photo that shows a boy named Chip Boyd in his Panama City, Florida, backyard enjoying the company of a baby gator purchased at Silver Springs. Young Chip wears a glove on his left hand, perhaps to limit the pain caused by the nips he expected from the alligator's pointy teeth. The girl who lived next door to me could have used Chip's glove, as we shall soon see.

Alligators start life at less than a foot long, making them seem like lovable pets, but those cute babies become enormous and deadly. Mature males can reach a length of about ten to fifteen feet and weigh up to a thousand pounds.

The alligator that took up residence next door to us never had the opportunity to grow to anywhere near that size.

One day the neighbor girl was in the yard admiring her pet when its jaws snapped down on her index finger. She shrieked and spun around, the alligator dangling in the air and desperately trying to hang on as if on the spinning witch's hat at our city park's playground. Fortunately for the girl, centrifugal force triumphed. The alligator lost its grip on her finger and went flying. The sobbing girl rushed inside her house to seek aid and sympathy from her mother, who by this point likely thought that a seashell or a coffee mug with the girl's name on it would have made for a better souvenir.

The alligator disappeared from our lives shortly after that. Rumor was that the family released it into a lake. If so, the pet likely experienced a short life, since Florida alligators and Kentucky winters are not the most compatible of nature's wonders. So yes, sometimes geography does matter—a lot.

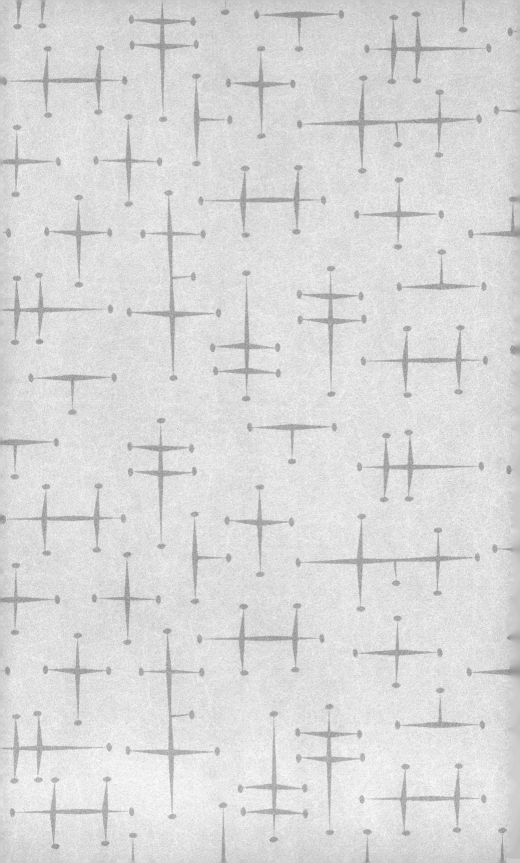

CHAPTER 11

I BORROW A PONY

I have never claimed to be especially skillful at bartering, yet one day when I was about eight years old I managed to make an extraordinary trade that gave me the use of an older boy's pony for an afternoon.

I don't recall what I gave in exchange to make this deal happen. In retrospect, I am certain the other boy came out on the better end of the arrangement, and he perhaps smirked as we shook hands on it. Maybe my negotiating skills did leave much to be desired after all.

For the longest time I had envied the few people in our neighborhood who owned ponies, and I dreamed of corralling one I could call my own. I identified greatly with the character Priscilla in the comic strip *Priscilla's Pop*, which I read each day in the *Knoxville News Sentinel*. Priscilla was a girl obsessed with the idea of owning a horse. She begged her parents relentlessly, but they steadfastly refused to budge. I empathized with Priscilla and admired that she often wore a cowboy hat to symbolize she would not easily give up on her dream.

A horse seemed beyond the realm of possibility for me because I knew absolutely no one who owned a horse. But two or three neighborhood children owned ponies, making that an attainable goal if my parents would only relent.

In the tradition of Priscilla's parents, they would not, so I settled for dime pony rides offered at the city park each year during Cumberland's Fourth of July celebration.

That is, I settled for that until the fateful day when I somehow finagled the deal of the decade. Sure, I would not own the pony, but it was mine for one entire Saturday afternoon, and I would not need to let someone else lead the animal as I rode, which was the case on the Fourth of July. With our deal sealed, the other boy led his pony to the pasture that adjoined the property my family rented, handed me the reins, and departed. I stood there, intoxicated by the moment. The pony stood there, confused but otherwise uninterested.

The animal looked glorious to me as I approached it. I lovingly stroked its side and tried to put my foot in the saddle's stirrup, conjuring an image of the Lone Ranger, Roy Rogers, or one of the many other cowboy heroes who entertained me on TV.

The pony stepped away, frustrating my effort.

I tried again. The pony stepped away again. I attempted a third time, and the pony, likely annoyed, walked slowly across the pasture, putting distance between itself and this intruding boy who clearly lacked essential equestrian skills.

This would not do. Leaving the pony alone in the pasture, I rushed up the nearby hill to the other boy's house. He was irritated that I interrupted his leisurely Saturday afternoon to help with what he viewed as a chore. The trade was done. Leave him be. But reluctantly, he returned with me to the pasture, boosted me onto the pony, and left without so much as a backward glance.

I was triumphant—momentarily.

The pony began to walk across the pasture—an excellent start—but then began to pick up speed, and I clung desperately to its neck. The pony never quite reached a gallop, probably not even close, but in a panic I swung my right leg around and slipped off, landing with a slight thud and a greatly broken heart, though no broken bones.

The pony, relieved of its burden, stopped to nonchalantly munch on grass. I sat several feet away, pondering my next move. This pony-riding reality did not match my cowboy-galloping-to-the-rescue fantasy in any way. I gazed back across the pasture and toward the hill, hoping to see the other boy and call him back for another boost and another try. But he was gone, and considering his attitude the last time, I did not dare roust him again.

Reluctantly, a failed cowboy, I moped into the house and in my misery found other things to occupy my time.

But my defeat was not yet complete. There would be an epilogue.

My father had been away from the house, but when he returned home, he immediately tracked me down.

"Do you know why there is a pony in the backyard?" he asked.

The backyard? I had left the pony in the pasture. What madness had the animal been involved in since I'd parted ways with it? Dad was not the least bit happy about his discovery and probably wouldn't have been that much happier if the pony had remained in the pasture. After all, no pony was supposed to be in either place.

Dad was about to grow even unhappier.

"I borrowed it," I confessed.

They say confession is good for the soul, but this is debatable if you are an eight-year-old boy guilty of temporarily adopting a large animal.

"You what?"

"I borrowed it."

I mumbled that last response, sensing that this extraordinary day that had turned into disappointment was about to take the next fatal step into disaster. Even at a young age, you arrive at moments when you know you've miscalculated. In my defense, while Mom and Dad refused to let me own a pony, they never explicitly forbade me from borrowing one. After all, parents can't think of everything their offspring might cook up.

> **Even at a young age, you arrive at moments when you know you've miscalculated.**

Dad didn't say anything else. Instead, he strode outside, grabbed the pony's bridle, and began to lead the stubborn beast back toward its owner's home. I scampered behind him, tearfully calling out apologies. Dad had recently injured an arm at the coal mine, and as I watched him struggle one armed with the pony, I feared he would reinjure himself and I would live my remaining years filled with guilt. But he finished the task unharmed, his bad arm in no way interfering with his ability to give me a stern lecture about responsibility, animal hazards, and common sense.

Eventually, the sun set behind the mountains, and this doomed day came to a welcome end. My longing for a pony was squelched once and for all.

CHAPTER 12

PURPLE-INK JOURNALISM, SUPREME COURT RULINGS, AND OTHER SCHOOL HAPPENINGS

On the first day of first grade in 1964, I woke up so excited about what the day would hold that I promptly threw up.

Carefully, I arranged the quilt and sheet to hide the incriminating evidence from my mother. I had awaited this momentous day for nearly as long as I could remember and did not plan to begin it with a thermometer under my tongue and my mother pressing her hand against my forehead, fretting over whether I felt feverish.

First grade was the real beginning of school for us in those days in Kentucky, as there was no mandatory kindergarten. For years I had watched Shelia trot off to Cumberland Elementary while I stayed behind to watch *Captain Kangaroo* on TV or play on the swing in our yard, loudly singing my off-key version of the popular Pat Boone song *Speedy Gonzalez.* I envied Shelia and longed for the day that I, too, could begin my formal education.

That day had arrived. I would not let illness—or more likely a temperamental stomach brought on by overexcitement—interfere. When Mom and Shelia set out toward the school that morning, I walked proudly alongside them, anticipating the extraordinary things that lay ahead and unconcerned about how Mom would react later when she made my bed.

The elementary school housed grades one through eight. Mom, Shelia, and I entered a cavernous hallway where chattering children and their parents darted about, faces appearing and then disappearing in a blur of confusion as I struggled to get my bearings. Just before we reached a water fountain, my mother tugged me through an open door, and Mrs. James's first-grade classroom revealed itself, a paradise of neatly arranged desks, a freshly cleaned chalkboard, and an inviting reading circle with benches.

Mrs. James beamed at me. "Shelia's little brother!" she exclaimed.

My identity firmly established, I found a seat and placed my pencils, writing pad, and jar of white paste on my newly claimed desk. Near me, a boy hummed the theme from *Combat,* a popular TV show about American soldiers fighting in France during World War II. I liked this boy instantly, appreciative of his taste in television viewing and his ability to calmly hum in tune with so much nervous commotion around him.

A couple of rows away, next to the windows, sat two African American girls, which was more momentous than I realized. It had been just ten years since the US Supreme Court's Brown v. Board of Education ruling that led to the integration of public schools, and much of the South was still ignoring or fighting that ruling. Kentucky had been somewhat different, and by 1964, 92 percent of Kentucky school districts were desegregated compared to about 20 percent in the rest of the South, according to the book *Freedom on the Border: An Oral History of the Civil Rights Movement in Kentucky*, by Catherine Fosl and Tracy E. K'Meyer.

Certainly, I could see that these two girls were Black and everyone else in the classroom white, but I knew nothing about court rulings or integration—or that not so long ago those girls would not have been there.

Another court ruling had also changed schools not that long before I arrived. In 1962, the US Supreme Court decreed that school-sponsored prayers were unconstitutional, which meant if Cumberland Elementary teachers had been leading morning prayers in their classrooms, that had come to a halt. Students were free to pray on their own, of course, but the school was to keep its nose out of their interactions—or lack of interactions—with God.

In truth, even with that court ruling, school didn't remain completely religion-free. My third-grade teacher, Mrs. Lisenbee, read to us most afternoons from *Aunt Charlotte's Stories of Bible History*, a book that used a framing device in which children asked their Aunt Charlotte questions about biblical characters, and the aunt then told them that character's story. I inhaled those tales, blissfully unaware that a potential constitutional violation was being carried out before my eyes.

Periodically, the school gathered us for assemblies featuring visitors from Camp Nathanael, a Bible camp in Knott County. I'm sure these were thinly disguised commercials aimed at enticing us to attend the camp, but from a kid's perspective, they did come with one saving grace. One of the Camp Nathanael representatives happened to be a ventriloquist. He always brought along his dummy, providing an extra measure of entertainment to the assemblies.

But those religious interludes were an aside. Mostly we concentrated on making friends, trying to stay out of trouble lest we become victim to a teacher's paddle, and, of course, studying the usual reading, writing, and arithmetic of elementary school academic lore.

In the early 1960s, the famous Dick and Jane primers were still a popular way to introduce children to the wonders of reading, but I never encountered them. Instead, Mrs. James instructed us in the finer points of phonics using books about a similar brother-and-sister duo, Tom and Betty, who served the same purpose as Dick and Jane but never gained equivalent fame and accolades.

Though they were cursed to dwell in the shadow of those other reading-comprehension siblings, I envied Tom and Betty all the same. Instead of a dog named Spot, they owned an English springer spaniel named Flip, a daring hero of the Lassie variety who once retrieved Tom's lost mitten and delivered it to his school. Tom also owned a pony that he named simply Pony, relieving us of the obligation to learn an extra word. Tom and Betty's books had titles such as *My Little Red Storybook*, *My Little Green Storybook*, *Under the Apple Tree*, and *The Little White House*. In one of their books, *On Cherry Street*, Tom, Betty, and their younger sister, Susan, encountered an organ grinder and his monkey.

> *Around and around went*
> *the little monkey.*
> *Tink-tink-tinkle, went the organ.*
> *"See the monkey dance!" said Tom.*
> *"We can give the monkey*
> *some money for his little basket.*
> *Then he will dance for us."*
> *Jingle, jingle, went the money*
> *into the little red basket.*

Imagine it. You walk down the street in your hometown, and an organ grinder appears, complete with monkey. That's something I could never hope to experience in Cumberland, so my mundane real life once again had been topped by the fictional life of Tom and Betty, despite their stilted language and everyone in their town's insistence on repeating simple words.

With inspiration from Tom and Betty, reading time became one of my favorite classroom activities, and I eagerly anticipated once-a-week visits to the school library. The librarian often showed filmstrips that taught us about such topics as Johnny Appleseed and his tree-planting efforts or James Fenimore Cooper and his Leatherstocking Tales.

Then we would browse the shelves and select a book to check out. Just one. But that was enough. Over the course of my elementary school years, I launched numerous expeditions into those shelves to discover such titles as *Matthew Looney's Voyage to Earth*, *Mystery in Longfellow Square*, *A Wrinkle in Time*, *The Blue Man*, multiple volumes in the Doctor Dolittle series, and a collection of Sherlock Holmes stories, among many others.

Once I stumbled across a copy of *Charlotte's Web* by E. B. White and triumphantly carried it to the checkout desk. My jubilation was short lived. Two eighth-grade girls volunteering in the library deemed me too young to grasp the complexities of advanced literature about clever spiders. They sent me back into the stacks to find something more suitable for, in their minds, my limited reading comprehension.

Dejected, I returned Charlotte and her pig friend Wilbur to the appropriate spot on the shelf. With my heart no longer in the search, I grabbed a random title as a substitute. I did at least make sure it was well below my reading abilities so I would experience no more trouble getting past the literacy security guards. Apparently, this book met with the eighth-grade girls' approval, and they magnanimously stamped it with a due date. In later years, I could easily have checked out White's classic, but *Charlotte's Web* had become tainted, evoking unpleasant memories, so I avoided it and satiated my reading appetite with other works.

A decade after I finished my years at Cumberland Elementary, I became a journalist, but you could make an argument that I launched my future career in Mrs. Creech's sixth-grade classroom. Another boy, who enjoyed writing as much as I did, approached me with the idea of publishing our own weekly newspaper. His enthusiasm was contagious as he laid out his vision. We could write articles about happenings around the school. We could create cartoons and comic strips. We could enlist the aid of other students in writing essays about topics that inspired them.

A decade after I finished my years at Cumberland Elementary, I became a journalist, but you could make an argument that I launched my future career in Mrs. Creech's sixth-grade classroom.

I instantly saw the brilliance of his plan as well as its major flaw. We had no way to print such a newspaper other than to stay up into the wee hours of the night crafting each copy by hand as if we were sixth-century monks dutifully recording the words of sacred texts by candlelight. That would be tedious and drain the enterprise of its fun.

We put our combined sixth-grade brain power to work solving this obstacle and arrived at an excellent solution. Mrs. Creech printed many of our tests on a ditto machine housed in a room down the hall. The ditto machine churned out as many copies as you liked in purple ink, which had a pleasing chemical aroma that we took a good whiff of before we began answering test questions.

If a purple-ink-producing ditto machine could print tests, it certainly could print a newspaper, or at least individual eight-and-a-half-by-eleven-inch sheets of paper that could be stapled together and serve our purpose.

Mrs. Creech approved our plan without hesitation, perhaps delighted to have two such enterprising young men under her tutelage. We named our newspaper *The Weekly Star* and sold it to our classmates and other sixth graders for a nickel. We used the proceeds to reimburse Mrs. Creech for those eight-and-a-half-by-eleven-inch sheets of paper. To my knowledge no copies of *The Weekly Star* survive, but I imagine it was an eclectic mix of dull school happenings, crude drawings, and occasional plagiarism. Still, we beamed with pride each week as the latest issue emerged from the ditto machine.

I do have one memory of *The Weekly Star's* actual contents. In addition to my writing and editing duties, I created a comic strip that included a dog inspired by Snoopy of *Peanuts* fame. In one two-panel strip, the dog was getting soaked in a thunderstorm and thought balloons informed readers of his grumbling reaction to his fate. In panel one, he thinks, *Here I am, out in the rain again.* In panel two, he finishes his thought: *All because that stupid artist can't draw a doghouse.* In sixth grade, I had not yet heard the term *breaking the fourth wall,* but I had accomplished it effortlessly nonetheless.

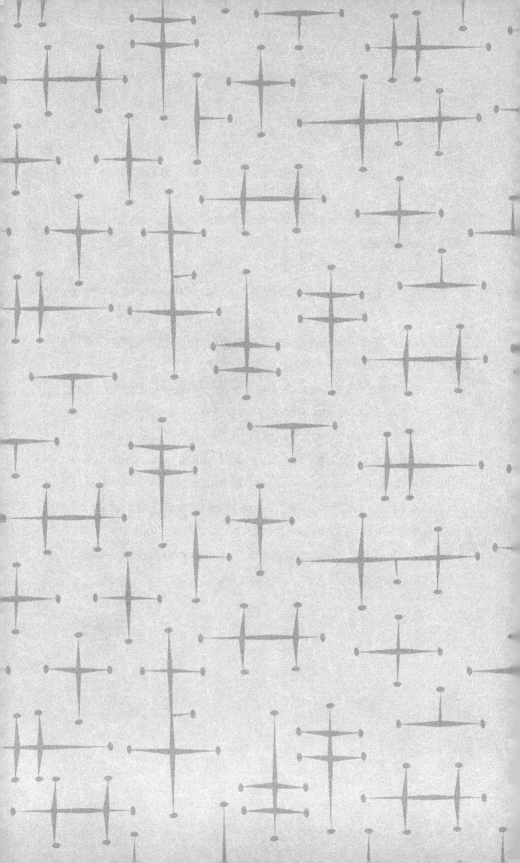

CHAPTER 13

MICKEY MOUSE, KING KONG, AND OTHER THIRTY-FIVE-CENT CELLULOID ESCAPADES

On a magnificent day in 1962, my teenage cousin and her boyfriend volunteered to take Shelia and me to the Novo, the one-screen movie theater in Cumberland. At least I think they volunteered. Perhaps they already had a date planned and my parents suddenly needed emergency babysitting help.

The details didn't matter to a four-year-old who had never stepped inside a theater. I knew I was in for an adventure, and that surmise proved correct as we entered the Novo, where rows and rows of padded seats faced a mammoth curtain. In a while, the lights dimmed, and the curtain parted to reveal an enormous screen. Likely we saw a cartoon and previews of coming attractions. Then the featured movie began. It was *Bon Voyage*, a comedy about a family embarking on a cruise. *Bon Voyage* starred Fred MacMurray, a familiar face to me because he played the father on one of my favorite TV shows, *My Three Sons*. I never saw *Bon Voyage* again, and I recall no details beyond what I've already mentioned, yet that two hours seemed magical, and I felt a little older sitting with my cousin and her boyfriend, basking in the glow of Fred MacMurray.

Through the rest of the 1960s and into the 1970s, I returned to the Novo many times to watch such movies as *King Kong vs. Godzilla*, *Planet of the Apes*, and *Soylent Green*. But some of the most memorable theater-going days happened around 1964 or 1965 when the Novo sponsored what it called the Mickey Mouse Club. This soon became a favorite activity for children on Saturday afternoons. I don't recall any actual connection to Mickey Mouse specifically or the Disney empire in general, so the club's name was perhaps just a way to lure us to the theater and separate us from thirty-five cents, the going rate for a child's admission ticket.

Along with a movie suitable for children, the weekly club featured dance contests and other activities held on the stage that jutted out from the screen. But perhaps the most memorable thing about the Mickey Mouse Club was this feature: We were treated to movie serials from the 1940s and 1950s. The first of these was *Batman and Robin*, a fifteen-chapter black-and-white saga from 1949 starring Robert Lowery and Johnny Duncan as the masked comic book crime fighters. For fifteen thrilling Saturdays, the Dynamic Duo battled an evil villain named the Wizard as I munched on popcorn and cheered them on. The soon-to-be-popular *Batman* TV series was still a year or so away from its debut, so this low-budget affair served as a preview of what was to come—although we didn't realize that at the time.

Years later, as a reporter for *The Tampa Tribune* in Florida, I wrote an article about movie serials and interviewed Johnny Duncan. He recalled that he nearly missed out on the role of teenage Robin because he was twenty-six and Batman creator Bob Kane had made it known that he wanted an actual teenager. Producer Sam Katzman instructed Duncan to "dress young" for the audition, and the subterfuge worked. "We never told Bob Kane I was twenty-six," Duncan said.

The Mickey Mouse Club lost some of its luster after the credits rolled on the fifteenth and final chapter of *Batman and Robin*. The next week the theater introduced us to the first chapter of a serial about a Pony Express rider. We loved cowboys, but we could see them nearly any night on TV. This Pony Express rider lacked the dazzle of costumed crime fighters and offered little that *Rawhide* or *Bonanza* couldn't provide.

Eventually, the Mickey Mouse Club dissolved and we turned to other Saturday afternoon pursuits. Few of those activities could compete with the enchanting memories we collected as a result of dance contests, the aroma of popcorn, and Batman and Robin poised to come to our rescue in a darkened theater.

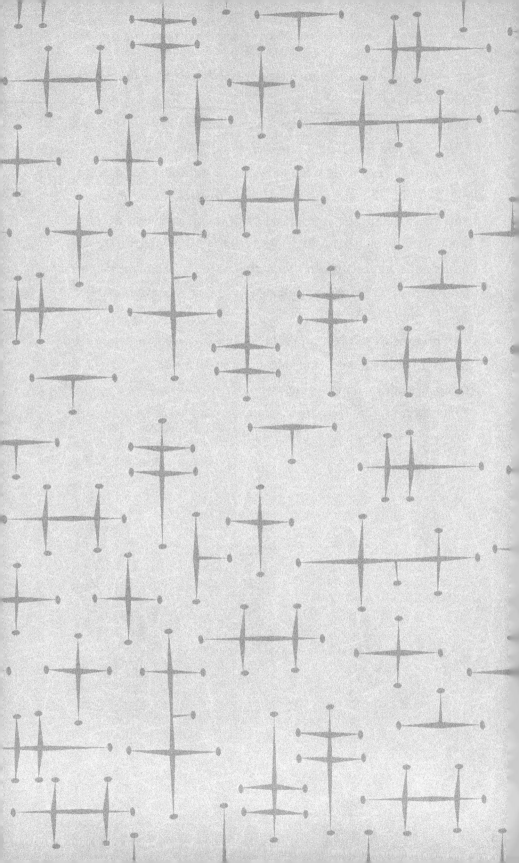

CHAPTER 14

THE CHURCH THAT BORE MY FAMILY NAME

◇◇◇

Each Sunday morning my family faithfully attended Blair Chapel, which might lead you to believe we possessed our own personal house of worship.

Sadly, this was not the case.

Blair Chapel took its name from the tiny community of Blair, which likely did owe its name to some ancestor of mine who helped settle it. Despite the fact that our family name matched the church's, we held no prominent role, although my mother did help teach Sunday school on occasion and sang in the choir.

Our denomination was Primitive Baptist. Later in life, when I told people I grew up in a Primitive Baptist church, they imagined I was making a clever joke about backward

> **When I told people I grew up in a Primitive Baptist church, they imagined I was making a clever joke about backward beliefs.**

beliefs. They expressed surprise to learn this was an actual denomination, part of a movement that arose in the early 1800s during a controversy over whether churches should support the efforts of missionary societies. The group that became the Primitive Baptists thought not.

Primitive Baptist preachers require no particular training, and in the case of Blair Chapel, they always had another job in addition to their funeral, wedding, and Sunday-sermon duties. Those sermons typically were blistering stream-of-consciousness oratories, with the preacher becoming more and more worked up about whatever message he desired to get across. Seminary-trained preachers usually present structured sermons, often with three critical points they want to drive home. They weave in an amusing or touching story—perhaps both—and wrap up the whole thing in twenty minutes or so, assuring that the congregation can leave in time to compete for the best tables at a favorite lunchtime restaurant.

Our sermons were more meandering affairs, with the spirit tugging the preacher in one direction and then another as the rest of us struggled to keep up. The sermon could last thirty minutes, forty-five minutes, an hour, maybe longer if the spirit had the preacher in a good throttle. I would look pleadingly at my parents, softly petitioning them to rescue us from the endless and, to me, confusing message. Usually, this resulted in stern looks, although on occasion they relented and whispered that I could sneak out early and visit my Uncle Butch and Aunt Edith, whose house was next to the church.

The preacher baptized the newly saved in a river that ran conveniently alongside Blair Chapel. He waded with them into the water until they were about waist deep. There he plunged the converted sinner backward into the flowing stream. Adults stood along the bank singing *Shall We Gather at the River*, but we children hustled onto a swinging bridge that spanned the river and watched the joyous occasion from above.

Sometimes my family skipped the main church service and just attended the Sunday school that took place before it. Some sources insist that Primitive Baptist churches don't believe in Sunday school, but ours did. Unlike the main service, Sunday school came with a defined time limit, so if things turned boring, you knew escape was not far off. Sunday school also concentrated on the kid-friendly Bible stories, such as David and Goliath, Noah's ark, and Jonah and the whale. Who cared about beatitudes ("blessed are the meek" indeed) when the mighty Samson was bringing an entire temple crashing down on his enemies?

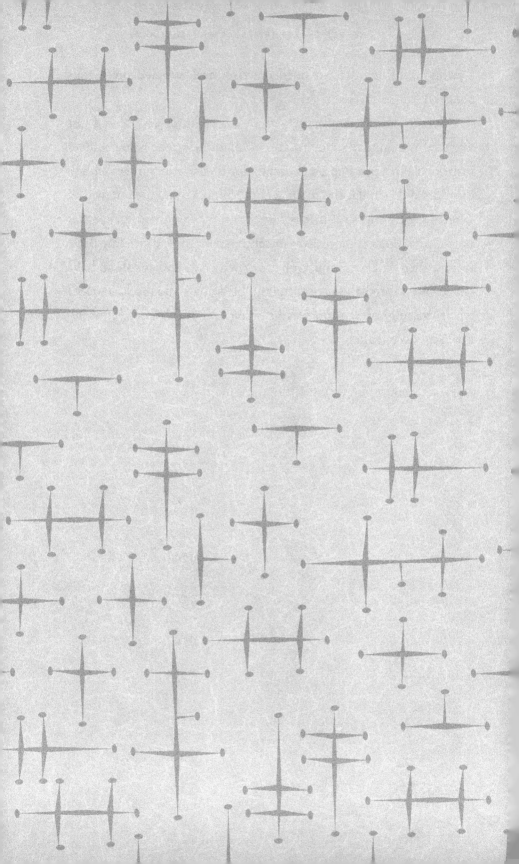

CHAPTER 15

SPACE GHOST GOES TRICK-OR-TREATING

For one of my earliest Halloweens, my mother—inspired by either her sense of humor or her resourcefulness—outfitted me as a girl. Like some cowardly first-class male passenger trying to sneak onto one of the Titanic's lifeboats, I wore a dress, most likely one Shelia had outgrown. This caused confusion for at least one older lady passing out candy to exuberant youngsters.

"Why isn't that little girl dressed up?" she asked.

"That's not a girl—he's a boy," my mother replied. "And he is dressed up."

The woman laughed, and if my costume had bothered me up to that point, it no longer did now that I saw how it fooled adults. Later at home I munched on candy and laughed at how my mother and I had tricked that lady—and probably many other adults who hadn't bothered to ask about the "girl" who wore no costume.

In the world of childhood, Halloween presented the extraordinary opportunity to experience frights (but nothing too frightful), to eat more sweets than stern adults normally allowed, and to prowl neighborhood streets long after the streetlights came on, something usually verboten.

Halloween also meant a "spook show" at the Novo, the one-screen theater in Cumberland. Spook shows now seem a remnant of a forgotten past, but at one time they were Halloween staples across the country.

Here's how they worked: The spook show began with a scary movie, perhaps with ghosts, vampires, werewolves, or some other malevolent creature that would put us—and our nerves—in the right mood. But the real event came after the movie's closing credits. A traveling magician took the stage (yes, there was a stage in front of the screen) and performed the typical magician repertoire of making items appear and disappear or sawing his lovely assistant in half. With each passing moment, we could barely concentrate on these impressive illusions because we knew terrors awaited us before the night ended.

And we were right. The magician's final trick always involved a Jekyll-and-Hyde type of transformation. He threw down a liquid-filled test tube or beaker, and smoke engulfed him as he bent over in agony, facing away from us. Then he turned with a snarl, revealing the monster he had become. We didn't get a good look, though, because the lights went out and the pitch-black theater filled with the screams of frightened children and teenagers. Illuminated dancing figures floated above us. Ghosts and bats mainly, I believe, but perhaps there were others as well. We knew they were the equivalent of cheap party decorations, but the buildup had achieved its goal and primed us for a fright. Year after year, the magician and his spook show delivered.

The community celebrated Halloween in other ways as well.

Cumberland High School sponsored a fall festival that featured carnival-style games and a haunted house with high school students dressed as monsters. One regular festival draw was Rosie, a fortune teller who erected a tent in the gymnasium and lured in all who were brave enough to learn what destiny had in store for them as foretold by a white-haired mountain woman.

Spook shows now seem a remnant of a forgotten past, but at one time they were Halloween staples across the country.

Spook shows and festivals aside, what we children really looked forward to was Halloween night and the opportunity to roam the neighborhood after dark, trick-or-treating.

In 1966, my favorite Saturday-morning cartoon was *Space Ghost*, which featured an intergalactic hero who flew like Superman, piloted a spaceship, and fired powerful beams from his wrists. As Halloween approached, I decided to trick-or-treat as Space Ghost.

I encountered a slight roadblock—or perhaps in honor of Space Ghost I should say force field. At that time, we bought our Halloween costumes at Hazen's 5 & 10. Eyeing that year's selections, I discovered that Hazen's sold a plastic Space Ghost mask but not a full costume, which I confirmed after thoroughly searching the inventory, searching it again, and then searching a third time for good measure.

My trick-or-treat plans were disintegrating like a spaceship targeted by a laser in a Space Ghost adventure. Then my mother came to the rescue.

"Let's get the mask," she said. "I can make the rest of the costume myself."

My outlook brightened. This was no idle boast. Mom was a top-notch sewer, quilter, and general whiz when it came to all things crafty. On Saturday morning she sat down with me as the cartoon's narrator, Gary Owens, intoned in his deep voice, "Spaaaace Ghooost!" and the exciting theme music blared from our TV. I watched enthralled as Space Ghost battled intergalactic villains while Mom studied his costume. Then she and her sewing machine went to work, the rat-tat-tat of the mechanized needle proclaiming each thread of progress. Soon she handed me the outfit to try on, complete with a cape to tie around my neck. I added my plastic Space Ghost mask, and staring back at me from the mirror stood Space Ghost—or a passable little-kid variation.

At school on Halloween, we always marched from classroom to classroom in a costume parade, showing off what we planned to wear on our trick-or-treat rounds that night. As we prepared for the parade, one boy regarded Mom's Space Ghost handiwork with approval.

"Where did you get that costume?" he asked in awe. Like me, he clearly was a Space Ghost admirer and Saturday-morning-cartoon devotee.

"My mother made it," I replied.

"Your mother didn't make that," he scoffed. "That came from a store."

But I knew the truth. That evening, as the neighborhood grew dark, Space Ghost set out on his latest adventure—a quest to gather candy and memories on a chilly October 31.

CHAPTER 16

NIGHTS BEFORE CHRISTMAS, SHEPHERD MISHAPS, AND A MISSING JOHNNY SEVEN

One Christmas, probably 1962, snow blanketed the hills and covered the narrow road leading to the house we rented. Shelia and I peered out the windows at our personal wonderland, excited at the thought that Santa Claus would soon visit our tiny abode deep in the Kentucky mountains. Ricky was too young to grasp the full magnitude of what was happening, but he would be the first that Christmas Eve to benefit from Santa's generosity.

Mom and Dad kept reminding Shelia and me that we needed to go to sleep if we expected a nocturnal visitor from the North Pole, but our overhyped minds refused to cooperate. As the clock ticked later and later, my parents' frustration grew, since they probably wanted some sleep themselves.

What occurred next remains a mystery. Something—we weren't sure what—was happening on the front porch. Did Shelia and I hear a sound? Did Mom and Dad tell us they heard someone rattling around out there? My parents crept toward the door, and I followed, unconcerned about the rush of freezing air that would penetrate my pajama-clad form when one of them tugged the knob to reveal the night's secrets.

Something lay on the other side of the door, but it wasn't a person. Sitting on the porch was a spring-mounted rocking horse, Ricky's gift from Santa, who had stood outside moments ago. I looked to the snow-covered road. Were those reindeer hoof marks leading away from our house, or small drifts transformed into something more magical by a four-year-old's overactive imagination?

Dad carried the horse inside as Mom reminded Shelia and me of a crucial Christmas Eve fact.

"Ricky is asleep," she said. "That's why Santa Claus left something for him. If you expect Santa to come back with your gifts, you better get to sleep yourselves."

We raced to bed. I tumbled beneath quilts and shut my eyes tight to will myself into a slumber, praying that Santa would not lose patience and give up on this house where two wide-awake children dwelled. Soon, sleep did overtake me, and as the final minutes of Christmas Eve ticked toward Christmas morning, Santa returned to finish his job.

To this day, the smell of citrus conjures Christmas morning images for me.

Christmas was childhood's most magical time, whether we watched breathlessly as the Christmas tree lights flickered on for the first time each year or searched the night sky on Christmas Eve to spot a red glow that assured us Rudolph was on the job at the head of

Santa's sleigh. We had no fireplace, so our stockings hung from tiny nails hammered into the wall. Santa didn't mind and filled them to overflowing with candy, nuts, and an orange. To this day, the smell of citrus conjures Christmas morning images for me.

The town of Cumberland celebrated by hanging decorations on light poles along Main Street. An annual Christmas parade included the high school's marching band playing Christmas music and Santa riding atop a fire truck and tossing candy to excited children.

Blair Chapel, the church we attended each Sunday, added to the celebration. Children in Sunday school classes drew names for a gift exchange that happened the Sunday before Christmas. That Sunday also featured children and teenagers singing Christmas carols in place of the adult choir. At the end of the service, deacons passed out paper sacks filled with delectable treats such as Cracker Jack, candy bars, and fruit.

The radio station, WCPM, invited children to write letters to Santa Claus and promised that Santa himself would read them on the air. We fired off our letters and listened faithfully each day as a radio announcer tried to raise Santa at the North Pole.

"Calling Santa Claus. Calling Santa Claus," he intoned, as if communicating via shortwave radio. Suddenly, the sound of a blizzard nearly drowned out the announcer, assuring us that he had broken through to Earth's most northern region. Then a hearty "Ho, ho, ho!" rang out from the radio. WCPM had made successful contact—once again! It was quite the thrill when the day arrived that Santa read aloud your letter and thanked you for the PS in which you promised to leave him milk and cookies.

As Christmas of 1963 neared, I longed for a Tiger Joe tank, a large battery-operated toy I saw advertised on TV. The boys in the commercial appeared to have a wondrous time with the tank, so I imagined with anticipation the World War II battles I could stage in our living room. The tank had a controller attached to it with a wire. You could move the tank forward or backward, and as it moved, a machine gunner atop the tank spun around and around, blasting imaginary bullets at an equally imaginary enemy. The tank also fired small plastic missiles at whatever unsuspecting pretend soldiers and buildings a child's mind could conjure. As I salivated over this amazing toy, I barely noticed an odd addendum at the commercial's end: "Sold at food markets only."

One day, perhaps a week or two before Christmas, Dad and I were in a grocery store in downtown Cumberland when I spotted, high on a shelf, a Tiger Joe tank in its box.

"Dad," I said excitedly, "that's what I asked Santa Claus to bring me."

Dad looked up at the toy, but I don't recall his response. When I awoke long before daylight on Christmas morning, though, the tank was there. Santa Claus never wrapped our presents, so I commenced playing at once, the roar of the tank and the rat-tat-tat of the machine gunner breaking the house's silence and awakening Dad from his holiday slumber. He suggested I wait until a more sensible hour to begin this racket, but Mom intervened, insisting that it was Christmas morning and I should be allowed to enjoy my present in all its noisy wonder.

When I was in sixth grade, I was recruited to perform in a school Christmas play. Oddly for a public school, the play was a straightforward telling of the biblical Christmas story, complete with Mary, Joseph, shepherds, wise men, and an angel. I played what the script referred to as "First Shepherd" and, like nearly everyone else in the cast, had one line: "In wonder behold him our savior and king."

Rehearsals played out to perfection, and on the day of the show, as parents gathered in the cafeteria where the performance would take place, the volunteer mother who directed the play gave us one last instruction. She would sit on the front row where we could see her from off stage, and to cue us, she would nod to each player when it was their turn to stroll out and say their line.

It did not go well.

The two other shepherds and I waited offstage for our big moment. But something went wrong. Our director looked in my direction and nodded. Or did she? It certainly looked like she did, but the script called for the angel to speak right before I entered and said my line, and the angel, who was already onstage near the manger, hadn't spoken yet. Clearly I was mistaken, so I stood still, waiting for the angel to take her turn.

Someone gave me a light shove. It was "Second Shepherd."

"She nodded toward you," he whispered. "That's your cue! Go!"

"But ..."

"Go!" he repeated.

Confused, I strolled onto the stage, intoning, "In wonder behold him our savior and king." The director's eyes widened. As I suspected, she had not nodded at me, at least not intentionally. The angel looked mortified. Her big moment had been stolen. There was no going back, so I took my place near the manger. Behind me, Second Shepherd said his line with great bravado and then took his place next to me. The angel looked plaintively toward our director as Third Shepherd uttered his line and completed our trio of bathrobe-clad Middle Easterners looking reverent before a mock manger, a plastic baby doll, and an increasingly perturbed angel.

The script called for the wise men to make their entrances right after the shepherds, but our quick-thinking director improvised. She nodded (an emphatic nod—no mistaking this one) at the angel, who looked relieved as she finally said her line. Of course, now the angel's line made no sense because she was addressing the shepherds, telling us to go see this baby we had already trotted out to visit. But it was the best move under the circumstances, and now the director nodded to the first of the wise men. The remainder of the play went off uneventfully, and later our parents praised the "flawless" performance.

We knew better, of course, and I avoided any postperformance banter with the angel. Fortunately, none of us planned acting careers.

Not every Christmas proved a winner. In 1966 I longed for a Johnny Seven, a toy gun made by Topper Toys and promoted as seven weapons in one, with such glorious functions as a grenade launcher and an antitank rocket. It was just what any 1960s child needed to defend the backyard from encroaching enemy forces. On Christmas morning I awoke early as always and sped to the living room to feast my eyes on my Johnny Seven.

But unless my eyes were deceiving me, the Johnny Seven was not there. I searched desperately beneath the tree, behind the couch, and anywhere else Santa in his haste might have inadvertently placed it. My first surmise was correct. No Johnny Seven.

Instead, my presents included a toy chest/shelf for storing assorted toys and books, a plastic bugle, a Fairy Tales book with Puss in Boots prominently featured on the cover, and a toy rifle that shot a puff of air. The rifle came with bubbles, so you could blow a bubble and then blast it out of existence with the air that burst from the rifle.

Really, it wasn't a bad haul.

It just wasn't Johnny Seven.

I am not sure why Santa failed to deliver. My parents were usually good about making sure I received whatever toy I placed first on my Christmas list. A year earlier, Santa had successfully delivered Duffy's

Daredevils, a longed-for toy that featured a motorized stunt car that you launched up a short ramp where it flew through a cardboard ring of fire then crashed into plastic yellow barrels on the other side.

Perhaps Johnny Seven was a hard-to-come-by item that year, the must-have toy for too many boys across the nation. Luckily, I was a stoic eight-year-old (at least in this case) and hid my disappointment.

Despite the Johnny Seven letdown, Christmas of 1966 was not without its merits. That year, the animated version of the Dr. Seuss classic *How the Grinch Stole Christmas* debuted, giving children something fresh to watch along with year two of *A Charlie Brown Christmas*.

Also, Kentucky enjoyed a white Christmas, never a guarantee. The snow began falling on Christmas Eve, and by Christmas Day the neighborhood and the surrounding mountains resembled the winter wonderland that singers always promised but the skies infrequently delivered. A 2015 article on the WeatherWorks website looked back at this monumental Christmas of 1966, when "an intense nor'easter not only blanketed coastal Virginia all the way to Maine with snow, but also lit up the sky with plenty of lightning and thunder." The storm left anywhere from four to ten inches of snow across southeastern Kentucky, providing a tiny bit of consolation for a disappointed eight-year-old boy. Trudging around outside, I discovered that when I fired my new toy rifle into a snowbank, the puff of air the rifle belched out left a satisfying indentation.

Santa Claus redeemed himself a year later, although by then I no longer believed, made cynical by 1966's unfulfilled expectations. This time, instead of a Johnny Seven, I longed for a Captain Action, a GI Joe–size action figure who could transform himself into any one of several superheroes. An extraordinarily accessorized toy, Captain Action boasted nearly as many clothing options as Barbie as well as a secret hideout and a car that doubled as a boat, allowing the good captain to take a spin around your bathtub.

As befitted the hero he claimed to be, Captain Action rescued my Christmas spirit, arriving under the tree with his car, his hideout, and his Batman and Spider-Man costumes. Outside of Hot Wheels and Matchbox cars, he was probably my last real toy, and Captain Action and my imagination enjoyed numerous adventures before he took a final bow and was shoved into a closet to lie dormant, if not forgotten, as the years sped up and left him behind.

CHAPTER 17

THRILLING TRIPS AND BACKSEAT NAUSEA

My parents' vacation plans always triggered competing emotions for me. I enjoyed visiting aunts, uncles, and cousins in faraway locales, such as Baltimore or Florida, and seeing what the world looked like outside our mountain community. But I suffered from extreme car sickness that even Dramamine could not keep in check.

On our trips to Maryland, I rarely made it to the top of Black Mountain before nausea kicked in and forced me to make use of the plastic bucket my mother thoughtfully provided in the back seat. By the time we stopped for breakfast on the other side of the mountain in Virginia, I was miserable, and likely so was everyone else in the car who had to endure my agony with me.

Beyond my personal woes, a mixture of geography and the time period made travel a tedious endeavor. Yes, President Eisenhower had signed the Federal-Aid Highway Act of 1956 two years before my birth, allowing the US government to begin building the interstate highway system. But in the 1960s, the system remained a work in progress. Regardless, the US Transportation Department had no intention of bringing the interstate anywhere near a secluded tiny town like Cumberland. Curvy and narrow mountain roads continued to provide our way out of the hills.

Even after we left the mountains, much of our travel involved driving on country roads and stopping for lunch at small-town cafes. When we finally reached a portion of the interstate, it was a revelation as we passed truck drivers or they passed us at dizzying speeds, the wind whipping through our car's open windows.

A car trip from Cumberland to Baltimore was nearly an all-day affair. By mid to late morning my carsickness would recede, and life in the back seat grew dull and tiresome as the miles passed without any clear evidence that we were close to arriving. Plenty of hugs and fun awaited us when we did, though. Baltimore was a mecca of uncles, aunts, cousins, and a grandmother, all from my father's side of the family. Technically, although we always said we were going to Baltimore, most or all of my relatives lived on the outskirts of the city in Dundalk, an unincorporated suburb with a population of eighty thousand.

The fact that my father had several brothers, one sister, and a widowed mother who ended up in Dundalk was not as extraordinary as it might seem. Before, during, and after World War II, thousands of Appalachian migrants poured into Baltimore and surrounding areas in search of employment opportunities they failed to find in places such as Harlan County, Kentucky. Even my parents lived there briefly as a young married couple, but they discovered that Baltimore life didn't sit well with them. Among other things, my mother complained about stepping over drunks who passed out in front of the entrance to their apartment building.

Although Baltimore was our top destination for vacation trips in the 1960s, my parents boldly decided in 1965 to take our summer excursion in a different direction—Florida. A year or two earlier, my mother's brother Irvin and his wife, Mabel, had moved from Kentucky to Lake City, Florida, not too far south of the Georgia state line. Since we now had relatives in the Sunshine State, my parents could not help but take advantage, even if the distance meant enduring extra hours of a carsick youngster in the back seat.

About the time my parents were planning our Florida trip, Walt Disney was busily and secretly buying land in and around Orlando for what would become Disney World, a prime vacation destination for families with small children. Unfortunately for seven-year-old me, the Magic Kingdom did not open for another six years. Luckily, like most Americans in the summer of 1965, I was blissfully unaware of Disney's plans and more than satisfied with the itinerary my parents had prepared. It included the Atlantic Ocean, glass-bottom boats at Silver Springs, performing dolphins at Marineland, and oddly enough, Old West gunfights.

The glass-bottom boats sounded intriguing and vaguely alarming. How would that glass hold up under our weight? What if it shattered? I didn't yet know how to swim. Fortunately, only a portion of the boat's bottom was glass—just enough to give us an aquarium-like view of fish swimming in the clear water below. The glass-bottom boats were a focal point of Silver Springs, which today is a state park but at the time was a commercial enterprise. Silver Springs itself is a natural phenomenon visited by humans for a good ten thousand years, dating back to the first Neolithic people in Florida, according to the state park's website. But the springs began attracting the tourist version of humans after the Civil War, and in the late 1870s two enterprising men attached a piece of glass to the bottom of a rowboat, and glass-bottom boat tours became a glorious thing.

The attraction became even more appealing after 1924 when two entrepreneurs acquired the rights to Silver Springs and perfected a gas-powered version of glass-bottom boats. This is what my family encountered when we arrived at the springs forty-one years later.

Beyond the natural wonders, I was fascinated to learn that Hollywood also loved Silver Springs and that scenes from six Tarzan movies starring Johnny Weissmuller were filmed there in the 1930s and 1940s. Those Weissmuller epics, such as *Tarzan Finds a Son* and *Tarzan's Secret Treasure*, provided some of my favorite TV viewing, inspiring hours of backyard tree climbing.

Next to Silver Springs was Six Gun Territory, a theme park that seemed out of place in Florida but ranked at the top of my list of favorites when Mom and Dad told us about the wonders we could expect to see on this vacation. The cowboy-themed attraction opened in 1963 at a time when TV Westerns such as *Bonanza*, *Rawhide*, *Wagon Train*, and *The Rifleman* dominated prime-time viewing. Six Gun Territory was the inspiration of a man named R. B. Coburn, who had enjoyed success with a similarly themed attraction called Ghost Town in Maggie Valley, North Carolina.

The park included forty Old West buildings, an Indian village, and can-can dancers in the saloon. A 2010 *Ocala StarBanner* article that reminisced about Six Gun Territory included this description: "The train ride from the entrance ... was routinely ambushed. Bank robberies happened daily, followed by shootouts between good guys and bad guys. Digger, the town's comical undertaker, was kept busy." Admission cost two dollars for adults and one dollar for children.

For a boy who engaged in his own Old West shootouts in the backyard, Six Gun Territory was nirvana. I drank in the ambience, covered my ears during the gunfights, and waited apprehensively to learn whether the train would be ambushed while we were aboard. Near the general store, Shelia, Ricky, and I clambered atop an unhitched buggy so Mom could take our picture with her Polaroid instant camera.

Six Gun Territory entertained tourists for two decades but closed in 1984. By then, TV Westerns had faded in popularity, and competing theme parks had risen to steal away tourists' dollars. When my family returned to Florida for a 1974 vacation, we gave the cold shoulder to Six Gun Territory and turned our sights on Disney World, opting for animatronic singing bears over gunslinging cowboys.

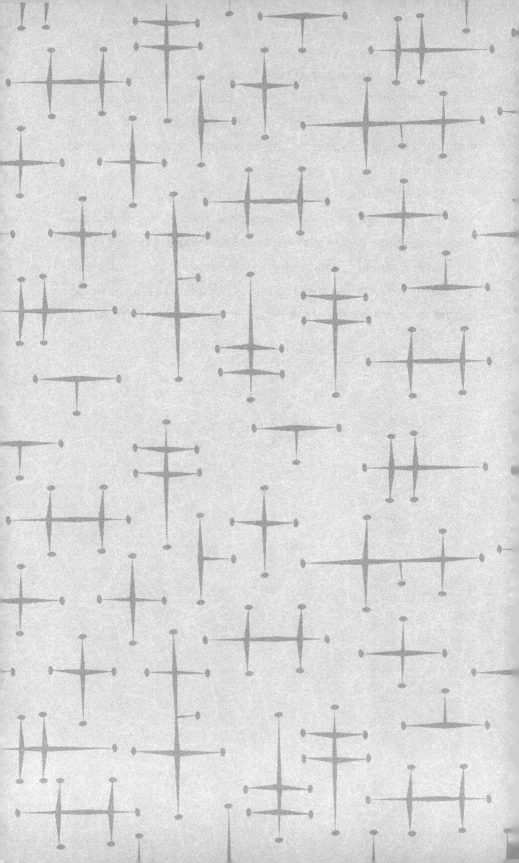

CHAPTER 18

BROUGHT TO YOU BY KELLOGG'S— AND A CABLE ANTENNA ATOP BLACK MOUNTAIN

Since we lived deep in the mountains, TV reception with an antenna was problematic at best, so in the 1950s a cable TV company opened in Cumberland run by a man named Bill Risden.

My parents, generally not ones for luxuries, signed up for this one, so we always had access to at least five channels that came in clearly—two CBS affiliates, two NBC affiliates, and one ABC affiliate. The ABC station was WLOS in Asheville, North Carolina, nearly 150 miles away. The other stations came from Lexington, roughly the same distance as Asheville; from Knoxville, Tennessee, about 120 miles away; and from the Tri-City area of Bristol, Kingsport, and Johnson City in Tennessee, about 60 to 70 miles away.

Only years later did I learn that cable TV was a foreign concept to many people living in cities. When my college roommate in 1976 crowed about his hometown of Louisville getting this wonderful new thing called cable, I was puzzled that he didn't already have it. He was equally puzzled that I had watched TV via cable my entire life. How could my tiny town in the mountains have been more technologically advanced than his big city on the Ohio River?

The answer lies in the whole reason someone invented cable TV to begin with. As television began to gain popularity in the 1940s, it became apparent that many areas of the country were too remote or too mountainous for TV viewers to pick up a signal with an antenna. That meant people in those locations lacked incentive to buy a television, a frustration for TV manufacturers.

This problem began to be solved in 1948 when cable was introduced simultaneously to communities in Oregon, Arkansas, and Pennsylvania, according to the California Cable and Telecommunications Association. "Community antennas" were installed on mountaintops or other high areas. My community's cable antenna was atop Black Mountain.

This magical device brought our family an enormous amount of entertainment and in my parents' view was probably well worth the price to keep three youngsters at least occasionally occupied. The three of us sat transfixed in front of the TV's glow as we watched such shows as *77 Sunset Strip, Wagon Train, The Rifleman, Bat Masterson, Dennis the Menace*, and *Car 54, Where Are You?* among many others. Commercials for products such as Kellogg's cereals and Campbell's soups punctuated the shows. We also saw plenty of pitches for Winston, Pall Mall, and other cigarette brands, memorizing catchy jingles ("Winston tastes good like a cigarette should") until someone in Washington decided the surgeon general was on to something with that warning about cancer. In 1970, President Richard Nixon signed a bill that banned cigarette commercials—and their kid-friendly jingles—from our airwaves.

Many Eisenhower Babies, myself included, never experienced life without television. TV sets were just another piece of furniture, no more extraordinary to us than a couch, a chair, or a table. In contrast, my parents' generation grew up without TV, and older baby boomers, especially the Truman babies, could tell weepy stories of that thrilling moment

> **Many Eisenhower Babies, myself included, never experienced life without television.**

when their family's first TV arrived and assumed its hallowed place in the home. But for many of us later boomers, the TV took its prominent role in the family before we did.

As it happened, television fit nicely into our nighttime lifestyles, which were ruled by the streetlights. When they came on, you came in, reluctantly putting that game of freeze tag on hold once again. If you were like me, to make sure you didn't miss a minute of prime time viewing, you took an early bath and maybe even went ahead and put on your pajamas. After all, you weren't going anywhere. The streetlights said so. Then you lay on the floor or settled into a favorite chair (mine was a rocking chair) and waited for *Flipper*, *The Monkees*, *Walt Disney's Wonderful World of Color*, or some other beloved show to begin. A few fortunate children owned color TVs, but most of us watched in black and white, missing the full impact of that historic cinematic moment when Dorothy steps from her gray Kansas farmhouse into the Technicolor land of Oz.

In addition to the standard fare of Westerns, medical shows, and detective shows, the networks gave us plenty of oddball bits of entertainment—a talking horse, someone's mother reincarnated as a car, a suburban housewife who happened to be a witch, a nun who could fly. The amount of inanity streaming from CBS, NBC, and ABC in the 1960s knew no bounds.

My mother tried to dissuade me from television's more intense offerings, such as *Alfred Hitchcock Presents, The Outer Limits, The Twilight Zone,* and *Thriller.* "You will have nightmares," she warned.

But I would plead, and she would relent.

Then I would have nightmares.

In truth, Mom loved the more frightening fare as much as I did. If one of the networks was showing *The Haunting* or *The Birds,* she tuned in, appreciative of a director's ability to conjure the right pacing, special effects, and musical score to give her a good scare.

On occasion, the cable would go out and we would stare mortified as Fred Flintstone, Lassie, or Napoleon Solo disappeared from the screen, replaced by "snow" that signified a lost connection. My parents assured us the cable company would soon solve the problem, and I imagined Bill Risden himself somewhere atop Black Mountain, perhaps in a horrendous storm, valiantly working to restore the picture to our woebegone black-and-white Admiral TV.

Maybe his effort wasn't quite as dramatic as the image my fevered childhood imagination conjured. But he always came through.

CHAPTER 19

ROY ROGERS, A BATTERED BROOM, AND ME

My favorite TV show in the early 1960s was *The Roy Rogers Show*, a 1950s series that CBS aired in reruns on Saturday mornings from 1961 to 1964. Roy was a cowboy who fought villains with the aid of his real-life wife, Dale Evans; his comical sidekick, Pat Brady; his horse, Trigger; and his dog, Bullet.

Roy and his pals appeared to live in a time warp that bridged the gap between the old West of the 1880s and the new West of the 1950s. Characters on the show dressed and acted as if they lived next door to Wyatt Earp in Tombstone, and Roy never went anywhere without his holstered six-shooter. Yet, anachronistically, the characters also enjoyed the latest in modern technology, communicating by telephone, flipping a switch to turn on lights, and driving cars when they weren't on horseback. Pat's cantankerous jeep, nicknamed Nellybelle, was practically a featured player, right along with Trigger, Bullet, and Dale's horse, Buttermilk.

This mishmash of centuries never diminished my enjoyment. I feared for Roy's safety when villains approached and cheered when Roy's sharpshooting and guile brought them to justice. Each episode ended with Roy and Dale singing the show's theme song, *Happy Trails*. The lyrics evoked a mood somewhere between happy and melancholy; this week's adventure was over, but we would do it all again next week.

The Roy Rogers Show fueled my imagination, and each Saturday afternoon I ambled into my hillside backyard to pretend I was Roy, confronting despicable bad guys with my trusty cap shooter and occasionally enlisting a girl who lived next door to fill in reluctantly as Dale Evans. My mother, ever tolerant of her son's daydreams but lacking a hobbyhorse, bestowed on me an old broom that my imagination transformed into Trigger. The battered broom and I traversed the yard at a gallop, outracing other imaginary steeds as we searched relentlessly for the next adventure.

Many years later I would meet my boyhood hero when I worked as a reporter for the *Daily Independent* in Ashland, Kentucky. Roy Rogers grew up in the area around Portsmouth, Ohio, where folks knew him by his birth name, Leonard Slye. In 1982, they invited Roy to come home for a visit, during which he would be honored with a parade and a VIP luncheon. Portsmouth was more than thirty miles from Ashland and technically lay outside my small newspaper's circulation area, but the city editor floated the idea of sending someone to the big event anyway, and I quickly volunteered. I wrote both a news feature about Roy's big day and an op-ed column recounting my childhood admiration for Roy. Here's an excerpt from what I wrote at the time:

> On this day, far from his Hollywood hills and far from my backyard, he was still a hero. Thousands of people lining a parade route whistled and applauded. "Hey, Roy," they shouted.

None of us called him Mr. Rogers. We had known him too long for such formalities.

Roy, his eyes twinkling, smiled back. The white hat, white boots, and silvery-fringed blue shirt he had donned left no doubt he was still King of the Cowboys.

Lots of older people, seeing Roy from a distance, marveled that at 70 he hadn't changed since his television days. I got closer and saw they were wrong.

His chin was no longer firm, his once strong legs were now spindly. His gait was no longer the sturdy stride that had once marched across a little boy's television screen nearly 20 years ago.

That didn't matter. Things have changed for both Roy and for us. He can't go back to the range, and we can't go back to the hillside. But we can all think about how much fun we had many years ago.

If the memories are somewhat rosier than the reality, that's fine. That's what memories are for.

Todays and tomorrows may bring tragedies and sorrows, but yesterdays will always be Saturday morning, a cup of cocoa, and Roy Rogers.

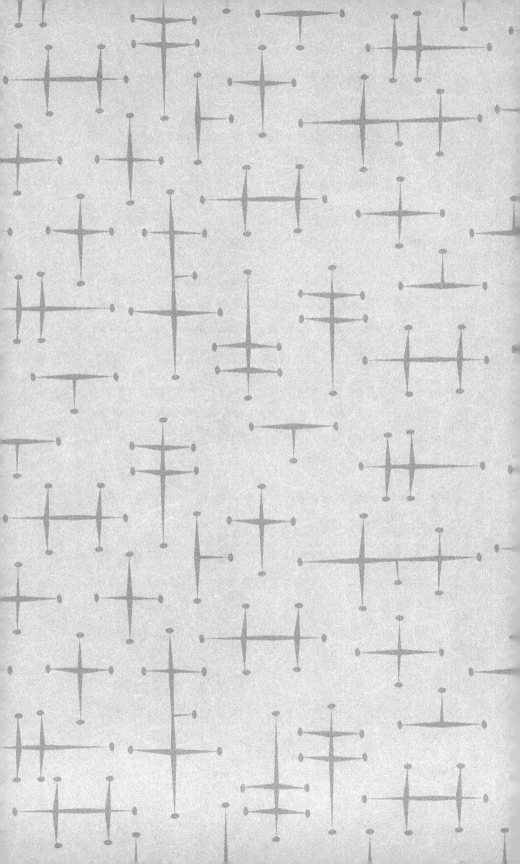

CHAPTER 20

THE SUPERMARKET THAT SWALLOWED A BASEBALL FIELD

In 1967, one of my friends excitedly announced he planned to try out for Little League baseball and suggested I do the same. The local Little League provided nine-to-twelve-year-old boys in Cumberland their only opportunity to participate in organized sports until they reached junior high and high school. Hesitantly, I approached Dad about allowing me to join the tryouts, fearful he might shoot down the request as an unnecessary extravagance.

"I guess we will need to get you a glove," he said.

This entailed a trip to a hardware store that offered a meager selection of sports equipment in the midst of its better selection of nuts, bolts, hammers, and wrenches. I eagerly tried on a slightly too big glove that bore the autograph of Willie Mays, the legendary San Francisco Giants outfielder who had played in the major leagues since

1951. Mays was known for his extraordinary fielding and was the reigning home run king among active players, but at this point he was in the latter part of his career. That season, he would hit twenty-two home runs, his lowest total since his first year in the league. This did not matter to me. I knew the name Willie Mays. I knew he was one of the greats. I smelled the leather and held the glove tightly as Dad paid the cashier. Back home I prepared for the tryouts.

The term *tryouts* was a misnomer. No one failed to make a team, but the tryout did give Little League coaches a chance to gauge our abilities, or lack thereof, in preparation for their version of a draft. The Cardinals selected me (I do not know in what round), and I quickly aligned my little-boy allegiances with the actual St. Louis Cardinals, which at the time were graced with such future Hall of Fame stars as Bob Gibson, Lou Brock, and Orlando Cepeda. Those Cardinals would win the World Series that year.

My version of the Cardinals also boasted a star athlete, a twelve-year-old named Leon Brown. Leon pitched a mean fastball, made amazing grabs as a fielder, and smacked the ball over the distant outfield fence. As an added bonus, he happened to be nice to us hapless nine-year-olds who stood lonely in the outfield, fearful that a ball would be knocked our way and disappointed if one wasn't. Leon would go on to star as a running back on the Cumberland High School football team and earn a scholarship to Carson-Newman College in Jefferson City, Tennessee. For me, he represented a first brush with athletic greatness.

Little League baseball also gave me my first taste of how progress could nonchalantly bulldoze over tradition and never look back.

Little League baseball also gave me my first taste of how progress could nonchalantly bulldoze over tradition and never look back. Soon after my first summer in the league, we fledgling baseball players learned startling news. Our beloved baseball field in Cumberland was slated to be demolished and paved over to make way for a Cas Walker Supermarket, a grocery chain with several dozen stores in Tennessee, Kentucky, and Virginia. The chain's crusty founder, Cas Walker, lived in Knoxville, where he served on the city council and often embroiled himself in controversy, such as in 1956 when a heated debate with fellow council member J. S. Cooper exploded into a fracas. *Life* magazine published a photograph of Walker with his fist drawn back, ready to slug Cooper as they tussled.

Walker's supermarket empire had grown steadily since he opened his first store in 1924. By 1967, as we Little Leaguers struggled to make double plays and track down fly balls in the outfield, Cas Walker and his chain set their sights on Cumberland and the one piece of land in the town's commercial district large enough to hold a store and a sizable parking lot. Our baseball field made for easy pickings. The construction crew could knock down a couple of dugouts, dismantle the backstop behind home plate, and get right to paving and building.

The Cas Walker Supermarket became a popular destination for Cumberland grocery shoppers, my mother included. Walker, the self-made millionaire, certainly knew what he was doing. But we nine-year-olds did not see a shrewd and knowledgeable businessman. Cas Walker was our Dr. No, whose evil emissaries had invaded our small town and carried out his diabolical plot to overthrow our childhood happiness.

Despite our gloom and our melodramatic take on Walker's business strategies, the end of Cumberland's Little League baseball field did not mean the end of Little League baseball. A field in the nearby town of Benham already hosted half our games and would continue to do so. The other half moved to Cumberland High

School's baseball field, which typically sat unused over the summer. The high school field came with an enormous downside. It did not have an outfield fence. Instead, the nicely trimmed outfield came to a sudden ignominious halt, as tall weeds had sprung up beyond it. The situation called for a special rule. Any batted ball that found its way to the weeds, whether it was hit there or rolled there, was an automatic double. Hitters could not race to third and home while outfielders frantically plunged into the savanna in search of the ball.

This, of course, meant that home runs did not exist at the high school field. At Benham, we could all watch in humble appreciation as an especially skilled and powerful twelve-year-old hammered the ball and sent it sailing over the fence. But at the high school, even Hank Aaron would have had to settle for a double, seething as the field's tightly governed rule kept him tethered to second base. Technically, on occasion some of us did make it to third base or even home plate off our hits, but only because Little Leaguers are notorious for their wild throws and poor catching. Hefty hitting couldn't get you a triple or a home run, but error-prone opponents could.

As time passed, we grew accustomed to the vagaries of the high school outfield rule, and even our animosity for Cas Walker dissipated. Perhaps we were surrendering to a world where adults called the shots. Perhaps we were maturing and becoming resilient young people who could endure any hardship and bounce back, all the better for it.

More likely, though, we just learned to enjoy the Lucky Charms breakfast cereal, Chef Boyardee pizza kits, and other delights waiting to be discovered inside Cas Walker's store.

CHAPTER 21

THE ARCHITECT, THE ENGINEER, AND THE MUMPS

In fifth grade, two of my close friends hatched a plan and included me in on it.

They wanted to build a fort near the riverbank on the appropriately named River Road, just down the street from where one of them lived. They even concocted a glamorous name for the proposed structure—Fort Riviera—which we all agreed sounded extraordinarily sophisticated.

I don't know what inspired the idea behind Fort Riviera, but the three of us had certainly read plenty of books in which adventurous boys created clubhouses, forts, or secret hideouts. Tom Sawyer, Huck Finn, and Joe Harper had even set sail on a raft, taking up residence on an island in the Mississippi River, where they aimed to become pirates. Surely we could design a fort on the edge of a much less intimidating stream.

Or at least some of us could. The other two boys had much better minds for this sort of enterprise than I did. One would grow up to become an engineer, the other an architect. We were in their element, not mine. My one emerging skill was the ability to string words together in a somewhat coherent message, but that meant nothing when it came to fort construction. In actuality, the two other boys plotted a structure more akin to a dugout or a lean-to than a fort, but this would work for our purposes. We would dig a wide hole three or four feet into the earth. Then we would gather fallen tree branches, trim off the excess limbs, and construct a roof over the hole, leaving a few feet of space to crawl through.

My one emerging skill was the ability to string words together in a somewhat coherent message, but that meant nothing when it came to fort construction.

The Architect and the Engineer assigned me a spade, and I put fifth-grade muscle into the undertaking. Years later, during one summer while I was in college, I worked in a coal mine, so this provided early training for the drudgery of manual labor. I proved an enthusiastic digger, even though I was slightly unclear on how this would pan out. Still, I felt confident that these two boys—the Frank Lloyd Wright and the Nikola Tesla of Cumberland—saw things beyond my visionary capabilities.

Digging a deep, wide hole takes time, but we had plenty of that in the afternoons once school recessed for the day, and certainly on weekends, so I did not doubt that at least the excavation part of our ambitious project could be completed with success.

But we weren't more than a day or two into the task when I began to feel ill, a development unrelated to my hole-digging efforts. My temperature shot up, my throat was sore, I felt weak, and alarmingly the left side of my face was swollen, mostly around the lower part of my jaw. The doctor gave a quick diagnosis.

"He has the mumps," he told my mother.

A vaccine that could have prevented this turn of events had been developed a year or so earlier, but I had not yet been vaccinated, and the virus took advantage.

My contributions to Fort Riviera, meager as they were, had to be put on hold. For the next two weeks, school was off limits as well, seeing as I would be contagious most of that time. Not that I felt like going to school. My body cried out for rest. Mom set me up with a pillow and quilt on the living room couch, where I lay watching TV shows such as *Land of the Giants* and *It Takes a Thief* when I didn't drift off into a troubled slumber. I mourned what I might be missing in my fifth-grade classroom at school as well as at Fort Riviera, but the mumps had taken such a hold that I cared only so much.

As my convalescence continued, I learned uplifting news. For some time, Mom and Dad had been saving money to buy Shelia, Ricky, and me new bicycles, and the day arrived to make the purchase—mumps or no mumps. I felt envious that Shelia and Ricky could hit the streets immediately while my moment of pedaling exhilaration was necessarily postponed.

But I still wanted to revel in the moment, so my parents rolled the bicycle into the living room, where, lying on the couch, I could admire its unmatched beauty. The bike was a Western Flyer model called the Wild One. It had curved handlebars, a black banana seat with thin white stripes, and one hand brake with a cable stretching from the left handlebar grip down to the front tire. Just in case that lone hand brake didn't provide enough stopping power, the bicycle also came with a coaster brake, probably a good call considering Cumberland's hilly terrain. The Wild One had a twenty-four-inch rear tire, a twenty-inch front tire, and what an advertisement described as a "psychedelic paint job" of "lemon-lime with shamrock green overspray."

The use of the descriptor *psychedelic* clearly identified the bicycle as one of the most modern models off the assembly line. That word was coined in the 1950s and in its most literal meaning refers to mind-altering effects brought on by LSD and similar drugs. But by the 1960s, *psychedelic* had been hijacked and was tossed around loosely to describe any distorted or bizarre images or sounds, including the flashy color schemes of bicycles.

Groovy, right? I was in awe.

The mumps ran their course, I was deemed no longer contagious, and on a Saturday one week after the arrival of my new bicycle I set out in the direction of Fort Riviera, determined to begin pitching in again on its construction. The world never looked so glorious as I turned the Wild One in all its psychedelic splendor onto River Road and pedaled toward the Architect's house. As I approached a curve in the road, I looked to my right toward the riverbank where a couple of weeks earlier three ambitious fifth graders had begun the construction of an ostentatiously named fort. Tree limbs partially obstructed my view, but there was no doubt about what I saw.

During my mumps-induced absence, the Architect and the Engineer had finished Fort Riviera, my contributions as unnecessary as I'd originally imagined. While I convalesced in front of a TV screen, waiting for the swelling and the fever to subside, they had dug, measured, sawed, nailed, and brought their vision to reality. Fort Riviera was a crude structure that city building inspectors would have frowned on, but to me on that sunny spring morning it was a majestic creation.

I rose slightly off the Wild One's banana seat and leaned forward, pedaling faster. I couldn't wait for the Architect to give me a tour.

CHAPTER 22

HANNA-BARBERA, SATURDAY MORNINGS, AND A BOSTON MOTHER WHO RUINED EVERYTHING

Robert Thompson, a Syracuse University professor who studies pop culture, makes the claim that five adults had the most influence over baby boomers. Two of those adults were our mothers and fathers. A third was Dr. Benjamin Spock, the pediatrician best known for his 1946 parenting guide *The Common Sense Book of Baby and Child Care*.

We children were largely unaware of Benjamin Spock, but we were well acquainted with the last two influential adults on Thompson's list: William Hanna and Joseph Barbera.

Hanna-Barbera Productions was responsible for some of our most beloved cartoon characters, such as the Flintstones, the Jetsons, Jonny Quest, Yogi Bear, Huckleberry Hound, and Quick Draw McGraw. Hanna and Barbera created the now largely forgotten *Ruff and Reddy Show*, one of the first animated programs made specifically for TV, as well as the popular *Scooby-Doo, Where Are You?* that spanned generations.

In the early 1960s, Saturday morning programming still gave us a mixture of cartoons and reruns of live-action children's shows from the 1950s, such as *The Roy Rogers Show, Fury, Sky King, National Velvet,* and *My Friend Flicka.*

That changed in 1966, a seminal year in the world of cartoons, superheroes, and children's programming. A comic book advertisement revealed that come September, CBS planned an extraordinary Saturday morning lineup of new cartoons: *Space Ghost and Dino Boy, Frankenstein Jr. and the Impossibles, The New Adventures of Superman,* and *The Lone Ranger.* Not all of those were Hanna-Barbera productions, by the way.

As often was the case with promotional material for 1960s TV programming, the advertisement specified that the cartoons were "in color," a cruel tease for those of us with black-and-white televisions.

Clearly, CBS was inspired by the success of the live-action *Batman* TV series that had debuted on rival ABC in January and captivated children on Wednesday and Thursday nights. CBS sought to capitalize on the superhero craze, and Saturday morning proved to be the perfect time to do it.

By the next year, all three networks joined this Saturday morning battle for children's attention, adding to our TV diets such cartoons as *Spider-Man, The Fantastic Four, The Herculoids, Shazzan, The Superman/Aquaman Hour of Adventure,* and *Birdman and the Galaxy Trio.*

I reveled in it all. Saturday mornings could only get better each and every year. I was certain of it.

What I didn't know was that a group called Action for Children's Television was hard at work with plans to disrupt my Saturday morning viewing. The group, led by a feisty mother named Peggy Charren, objected to the violence in these cartoons. In a 2015 obituary for Charren, the *New York Times* described her as "an inveterate cajoler, persuader, petitioner, testifier, public speaker, and letter writer."

The *Times* wrote, "[Charren] took up her crusade in the 1960s, when she was rearing two young daughters in a Boston suburb and was frustrated by what she saw on television for them—rampant advertising for toys and sugary cereals and, as she once put it, 'wall-to-wall monster cartoons.'"

Yes, she opposed every single thing I adored about Saturday mornings. Middle-aged Peggy Charren and ten-year-old me clearly saw the world differently.

Sometime in 1968, as I anticipated the next episode of *The Herculoids*, Charren and a group of like-minded mothers gathered in her Massachusetts living room to plot against me. They began to lobby lawmakers, network executives, and anyone else they could get to listen, making the argument that children's television should be less violent and more educational. Fewer explosions. More uplifting fare. Their progress was slow but effective.

Evidence of early victories came in the fall of 1968. Instead of a new round of violent action-adventure shows, we were greeted with lighthearted cartoons such as *Wacky Races*, *The Go-Go Gophers*, and *The Archie Show*. At least Archie was a comic book character I enjoyed, even if he didn't fire powerful beams from his wrists to destroy his enemies. Instead, he was a teenager who engaged in humorous teenage escapades with his pals, and he had been doing so since 1941, making for an extraordinarily extended adolescence.

One saving grace in the new Saturday morning lineup was *The Batman/Superman Hour*, a successor to the previous year's *Superman/Aquaman Hour of Adventure*. At least for those sixty minutes we could witness superhero rough-and-tumble and perhaps an explosion or two.

Despite the best efforts of fretful adults, children's love of violent entertainment never truly went away, as evidenced by the later rise of video games that allowed young people to shoot, blow up, or pound away at any number of virtual targets. A new generation of adults took its turn at tsk-tsking at how children were doomed, although if we were honest we would have admitted that the only thing that kept 1960s children from being addicted to violent video games is that they weren't available.

Peggy Charren, her cadre of meddling mothers, and subsequent anxiety-ridden adults had not been triumphant after all.

CHAPTER 23

THE CASE OF THE RELENTLESS READER

Books weren't that easy to come by in my hometown, but the community did boast a gem of a building that became one of my favorite hangouts—the Rebecca Caudill Public Library.

The town named the library in honor of a children's author born in Cumberland in 1899 when the community was still called Poor Fork. Rebecca Caudill wrote more than twenty books, including *Tree of Freedom*, a 1950 Newbery Honor Book, and *A Pocketful of Cricket*, a 1964 Caldecott Honor Book. For me, though, Rebecca Caudill was the name of a building, and that building held enchantment.

On an otherwise dull Saturday afternoon, I could entertain myself by examining the titles on the spines of a seemingly endless supply of reading material. I would pluck from the shelves a biography of Stephen Foster or a copy of Jules Verne's *Around the World in 80 Days* and dedicate the remainder of the day to immersing myself in a book's pages, roused only when my parents reminded me it was my night to wash dishes.

I was an inveterate reader, inspired at an early age by *Green Eggs and Ham*, by Dr. Seuss; *Benjamin in the Woods*, by Eleanor Clymer; *Stop That Ball*, by Mike McClintock; and a handful of other books for beginning readers that found their way into our house. Over time, as my reading abilities improved and Benjamin's adventures in the woods grew tedious through repeated visits, I discovered the Henry Huggins series by Beverly Cleary, the Doctor Dolittle series by Hugh Lofting, and assorted other wonders.

I came across those book series on my own, but it was my aunt Mabel who introduced me to the series that captured my imagination like no other—the Hardy Boys.

Mabel was married to my mother's brother Irvin. One Christmas (probably 1965) Mabel mailed gifts to Shelia, Ricky, and me from her home in Lake City, Florida. I tore the wrapping off mine to reveal a book with a captivating cover. It showed a beach with waves lapping near the entrance to a cave. A white-haired man—somehow menacing, even though there was nothing specific you could point to that would confirm this—walked toward the cave. His head was slightly turned to the left, as if he was about to look over his shoulder. He had reason to do so. Some distance away, two teenage boys crouched behind a large rock, spying on him.

The book was titled *The Secret of the Caves*. The author was Franklin W. Dixon, and over the next several years I came to view Mr. Dixon as the greatest literary gift to the world since Mark Twain and Charles Dickens. Later still, I learned that Mr. Dixon did not exist but was simply a house pen name used by numerous writers. Above the book's title were printed the words *The Hardy Boys*. Clever even at age seven, I deduced that the two teens hiding from that menacing man were those self-same Hardys.

Clearly, adventure awaited within these pages.

I began to read chapter 1, titled "Telescope Hill Trouble."

"Don't kid me, fellows," chubby Chet Morton said, moving his metal detector about the Hardys' front lawn. "You can find all kinds of swell things on the beaches with this gadget."

"Like what?" blond-haired Joe asked, winking at his brother Frank.

"Lost jewelry, money, gold-plated pens—"

I was right. Adventure did await me in these pages. Unfortunately, the wait would become a long one. I read several more pages, but alas, *The Secret of the Caves* was a 175-page novel, much longer than anything I had read to that point. I understood all the words. I could follow the plot. But the book's thickness proved too daunting for my seven-year-old attention span. I tried a few other times over the next year or so but could not maintain my momentum much beyond the first chapter or two.

Until 1967.

One day the nine-year-old version of me rediscovered *The Secret of the Caves*. By then I had conquered those Henry Huggins books, having read such titles as *Henry and the Clubhouse* and *Henry and the Paper Route*. The Henry Huggins books were nearly Hardy length, so I vowed that this time I would prevail over *The Secret of the Caves* and its intimidating twenty chapters. And prevail I did, right up until the final words when Mr. Franklin W. Dixon promised me further adventure in the Hardys' next escapade, *The Mystery of Cabin Island*.

Now that I had triumphantly immersed myself in *The Secret of the Caves*, I turned to the back cover, where the publisher, Grosset and Dunlap, had thoughtfully provided a lengthy list of Hardy Boys books then in print. I took in the delicious sounding titles: *What*

Happened at Midnight, The Disappearing Floor, The Clue of the Screech-ing Owl. "All boys from 10 to 14 who like lively adventures, packed with mystery and action, will want to read every one of the Hardy Boys stories listed here," began a paragraph that introduced the list. Ages ten to fourteen? I had broken through at nine, tasting forbidden fruit meant for older boys. This bit of lawlessness on my part was thrilling in and of itself.

Right above the forty-five titles listed, which included the intrigu-ing-sounding *Hardy Boys Detective Handbook*, the back cover posed a question that could be interpreted as simply curious or vaguely accusatory: "How many of these books do you own?"

One, I thought dejectedly.

And frankly, I did not see how I would ever obtain the others. Cumberland did not have a bookstore, and the Rebecca Caudill Public Library did not carry any of the Hardy titles, though to its credit, the library eventually remedied that oversight. The back cover of *The Secret of the Caves* failed to reveal its greatest secret: how to acquire these books if you lived in a small mountain town far from the kind of literary haunts frequented by people such as Mr. Franklin W. Dixon.

I could not rely on generous Aunt Mabel to mail more books from that great metropolis of Lake City, Florida, which apparently did have a bookstore. Acquiring those Hardy Boys adventures appeared impossible. Thank goodness the Rebecca Caudill Public Library could still supply me the remaining Henry Huggins books I had not read, and the school library had a nice run of those enchanting Doctor Dolittle books I quickly devoured. But (sigh) Frank and Joe Hardy— who owned a motorboat, piloted planes, and traveled to exotic locales to apprehend smugglers and counterfeiters—were much greater pals for a bookworm mountain boy than Henry and the good doctor, as wonderful as those two proved to be.

Fortunately, fate intervened. Or, more specifically, the Sears *Wish Book* intervened.

Every fall, the *Wish Book* landed at our doorstep in all its weighty wonder, bringing page after page of enchanting toys that Shelia, Ricky, and I could flip through and salivate over in search of items to add to our Christmas lists. When the 1967 catalog arrived, I thumbed through as always, carried away with delight by this beloved harbinger of Christmas. I turned a page and couldn't believe what I saw.

> **Every fall, the *Wish Book* landed at our doorstep in all its weighty wonder, bringing page after page of enchanting toys.**

Sears sold Hardy Boys books. Within the pages of that magical annual catalog was listed nearly every title that appeared on the back cover of my copy of *The Secret of the Caves*. The books were priced at ninety-nine cents each, but I immediately noticed a bargain I could exploit. A $2.67 "starter set" gave you the first three books in the series—*The Tower Treasure*, *The House on the Cliff*, and *The Secret of the Old Mill*—for one reduced price. "Follow the exciting adventures of two young detectives," Sears suggested, as if I needed any coaxing.

In all my years of wishing my way through the *Wish Book*, how had I never noticed the Hardys before?

No matter. The starter set found its place on my Christmas list, and on Christmas morning I sat on the floor next to the tree, admiring the cover art on the three volumes and inhaling the intoxicating aroma of new books. I immersed myself in *The Tower Treasure* while munching on candy from my stocking. "Chapter 1. The Speed Demon. Frank and Joe Hardy clutched the grips of their motorcycles and stared in horror at the oncoming car."

The *Wish Book* also introduced me to another favorite series, Alfred Hitchcock and the Three Investigators. Like the Hardys, the Three Investigators solved mysteries, but they came with a gimmick. Real-life movie director Alfred Hitchcock acted as their sponsor. Hitchcock—or at least a fictional version of Hitchcock—wrote introductions for each book and often appeared as a character within the pages as he arranged for the investigators to meet people who needed their sleuthing help with cases such as *The Secret of Terror Castle*, *The Mystery of the Fiery Eye*, and *The Mystery of the Screaming Clock*.

Thanks to the Hardy Boys and the Three Investigators, mysteries became my go-to genre. Any author could seize my attention simply by putting words such as *mystery*, *secret*, or *clue* in a book's title. I read *Mystery in Longfellow Square*, by Mary C. Jane; *Mystery of the Green Cat*, by Phyllis Whitney; *The Silver Spoon Mystery*, by Dorothy Sterling; and too many others to list or, for that matter, to remember. I discovered other series that featured young sleuths, such as Brains Benton, Trixie Belden, and Nancy Drew. I dreamed of becoming a detective, and my friends and I formed amateur detective agencies, longing for a good mystery to solve but never encountering any smugglers, counterfeiters, or international spies in our tame Kentucky town. What we needed was a sponsor like Alfred Hitchcock. Rod Serling might have fit the bill, but he was frustratingly unavailable in California.

One chilly morning a few of my pals and I felt certain we had stumbled upon a genuine mystery when we saw smoke billowing from an abandoned shed that stood on a hillside leading into the woods near my house. We investigated, crawling surreptitiously through the weeds in Hardy Boys fashion. Alas, the "villains" holed up inside the shed turned out to be teenagers on a camping expedition. They cheerfully invited us inside. We had solved the mystery of the abandoned shed, but at a price, our sleuthing spirits dampened perhaps permanently by the pedestrian reality revealed behind a seemingly strange occurrence that had sparked our imaginations.

As the years passed, I became painfully aware of the formulaic approach to each Hardy Boys story, and my fondness for them dulled. Soon after the Hardys' newest adventure, *Danger on Vampire Trail*, found its way beneath my Christmas tree in 1971, my allegiance to Frank and Joe was gone, and I focused my literary interests elsewhere.

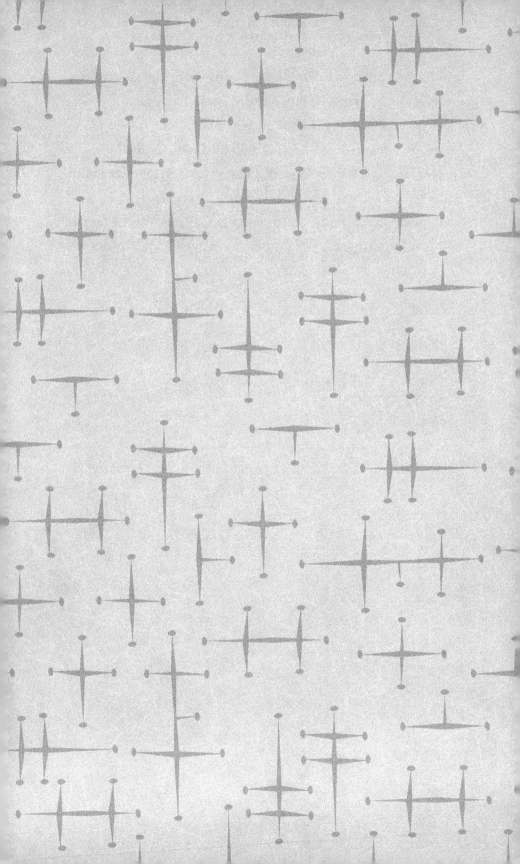

CHAPTER 24

THE WORLD INTRUDES

One day when I was five, I noisily bounded down the stairs of our Jackson Hill home and saw my mother and father huddled over our large black radio. Mom glanced up and shushed me, causing me to stop apprehensively halfway down the stairs.

"What's the matter?" I asked.

Mom did not mince words, despite my delicate age.

"Someone shot President Kennedy," she said.

I knew about President Kennedy, even if I was fuzzy on the details of what a president did all day. But I understood he was the country's leader, because I saw him on the TV news broadcasts my parents watched. At some level, I grasped the gravity of November 22, 1963. At another level, though, the president's assassination was something that happened far away and didn't directly infiltrate my world, which most days extended no farther than the backyard.

> Mom did not mince words, despite my delicate age. "Someone shot President Kennedy," she said.

I returned to playing.

My parents, presumably, stayed by the radio until Dad's ride to the coal mine arrived. That's the reason Mom and Dad listened to the assassination report on the radio rather than watch it on TV. Dad carpooled with other coal miners. The car that picked him up arrived by way of a narrow road behind our house, and he watched for that car from the kitchen window. That window happened to be near where we kept the radio, so Dad could stay abreast of the updates about Kennedy while keeping his eyes peeled for his ride's arrival.

That Friday began a dramatic week for the nation. Lyndon B. Johnson was hastily sworn in as the new president, the third of my short lifetime. Lee Harvey Oswald, the suspected assassin, was gunned down on live TV as detectives escorted him through the basement of the Dallas Police Department. President Kennedy's funeral dominated TV on Monday, and a mourning nation watched his son, John Kennedy Jr., salute the coffin.

I repeatedly pressed my parents on why someone would shoot the president, but they failed to offer a suitable answer other than to observe that some people are just bad. Still, this explanation likely sufficed for my five-year-old mind, because I watched plenty of TV detective shows and Westerns that neatly separated good guys from bad guys.

President Kennedy's assassination was the first major news event to leave its imprint on me, but many more punctuated my childhood and teen years. Mostly they lay on the periphery of my daily routine, even when they were historic moments with implications that would reverberate through the decades.

The evening of April 4, 1968, I turned our TV to channel four, which brought me the ABC network, a favorite on Thursday nights.

The lineup included *Batman, The Flying Nun, Bewitched,* and *That Girl.*

Sometime that evening, likely near the end of *The Flying Nun* or the beginning of *Bewitched,* a news bulletin interrupted the programming. A somber voice announced that Dr. Martin Luther King Jr. had been shot in Memphis.

At age ten, I was not exactly a news junkie, although the evening TV news played in our house each day and the *Knoxville News Sentinel* showed up at our doorstep every afternoon. TV news mainly meant boring newscasters droning on about boring grown-up things, so I gave Walter Cronkite, David Brinkley, Chet Huntley, and the others only cursory attention. I did find value in the newspaper, but mainly because it brought me comic strips such as *The Family Circus, The Ryatts, Snuffy Smith,* and others. I typically ignored the front page.

As a result, King's name, sad to say, meant nothing to me. I initially thought a random medical doctor in Memphis had been the unfortunate victim of a crime, a sorrowful enough prospect on its own merits but not one I would imagine to be of earth-shaking consequence to the world at large. Soon it became clear to me that this particular doctor was no random person and that, once again, American history had been forever altered by an assassin.

The year would get no better.

One morning a couple of months later, I awoke and turned on the TV, expecting to start the morning with a little cartoon frivolity. A news report greeted me instead, bringing grim tidings. Presidential candidate Robert F. Kennedy, brother of the slain president, had been shot to death in California. I watched, mesmerized that such a thing had happened again. Unlike with King, I was at least aware of Kennedy, if only because I still had fresh memories of his brother.

When my father awoke, it was my turn at the world-weary age of ten to share the distressing news about another assassination.

Some major events were ongoing rather than the sudden "we interrupt this broadcast" breaking-news variety.

One day I rushed home to ask Dad about something a friend had told me.

"Is the United States at war?"

I imagine I caught him off guard, but he acknowledged the country was at war in an Asian country called Vietnam. This was about 1966 or 1967 when I was eight or nine. Somehow, I had managed to live life oblivious to the war that was tearing the country apart. For me, war was something that had happened long ago, portrayed by actors on TV. I had to face the sobering reality that one was happening now, in my present time, and with real people.

Protests about American involvement in Vietnam started as early as 1963, when the United States just had military advisors in that country. But the likely reason the war had now come to my attention is that in 1966 the Selective Service upped the ante for draft-eligible young men. The government revised the draft policy to allow for the possibility that some college students at the bottom of their class rankings could lose their deferments. Protests grew in number and in fervor at colleges across the country, making the war difficult to ignore, even for an eight-year-old boy who lived nine thousand miles from Vietnam. Older Americans grumbled about "hippies" as young people objected to the notion that they should die for abstract reasons in a jungle on the other side of the world.

Even our music-listening habits couldn't shield us from the war. Along with pop songs such as *ABC*, by the Jackson 5, or *Ain't No Mountain High Enough*, by Diana Ross, we listened to protest songs such as *Fortunate Son*, by Credence Clearwater Revival; *War*, by Edwin

Starr; and *Ohio*, by Crosby, Stills, Nash & Young. The latter was about the Kent State massacre, where in May 1970 National Guard troops clashed with rock-throwing protestors at Kent State University in Ohio. The troops opened fire, killing four students, including two who were uninvolved in the protest.

By the time I reached high school in 1972, I had friends who vocally opposed the war. Some wore POW bracelets that were first created in 1970 by a student group in California. Each bracelet was engraved with the name of an American captured or missing in Vietnam, along with the date the person had been taken prisoner or had disappeared. The idea was that you would wear the bracelet until that serviceman, or their remains, had been returned to the United States.

Not all news proved as disturbing as assassinations and war.

My childhood coincided with one of the most daring exploration periods in history as the United States and the Soviet Union competed to become the first country to land people on the moon. I often sat on the floor in front of our TV to watch NASA's Gemini and Apollo launches, impatient for the countdown to commence and bored by newscasters droning on as they, too, waited for the rocket to blast away from the tower.

Space travel and speculation about what the future would be like played a significant role in our lives in the 1960s, and it went beyond real astronauts courageously boarding those rockets. On TV we watched *Star Trek* and *Lost in Space*. Commercials promoted Tang, the official drink of the astronauts, or so we were told. Our toys included Matt Mason, a six-inch-tall bendable-figure astronaut who came with space-exploration accessories and bendable-figure astronaut pals.

On the night of July 20, 1969, my family gathered in front of our TV to watch the faint, somewhat eerie image of Neil Armstrong descending the lunar-module ladder to set foot on the moon.

"It's like watching a movie," Mom said, perhaps in awe of how in her mere forty-five years on the planet the nation had advanced from trying to survive the Depression to spending a fortune to land these men on Earth's only natural satellite.

Next stop Mars, I thought. But my eleven-year-old brain had no concept of the distance to Mars and the additional time, effort, and technology such a journey required. Soon after Neil Armstrong and Buzz Aldrin completed their historic walk, many of my friends and I grew indifferent to the Apollo missions. Going to the moon remained cool—just not "oh, my gosh, I can't believe this is happening" cool.

In April of 1972, when I was in eighth grade, teachers pulled us from our normal classroom work to watch Apollo 16 astronauts John Young and Charles Duke explore the lunar surface. By now the astronauts had an electric-powered lunar-roving vehicle—essentially a moon buggy—that allowed them to drive several miles from their landing site. We jaded thirteen- and fourteen-year-olds, raised on rocket launches and lunar excursions, remained unimpressed.

One exasperated teacher turned to another.

"How can they be so bored by this?" she asked. "They take it for granted."

We could not argue. We did at least appreciate that Young and Duke gave us a momentary reprieve from memorizing historic dates, calculating square roots, and enduring another lecture about the placement of commas.

Go, moon buggy, go.

CHAPTER 25

DEAR COMIC BOOK EDITOR

Comic books played a minor role in my life until 1966. Two weeks into that year I turned eight, and, more significantly, the *Batman* TV series starring Adam West and Burt Ward premiered on ABC.

The series used a simple formula. Each Wednesday evening, Batman and Robin encountered a colorful villain who, in less than thirty minutes, trapped the Dynamic Duo in some diabolical situation that meant certain death. The episode would end with the narrator exhorting us to tune in the next evening to learn of their fate, "same Bat-Time, same Bat-Channel."

We faithfully returned for Thursday's exciting escape and finale.

Suddenly, kids in my neighborhood, myself included, couldn't get our hands on enough comic books. The Rexall drugstore in town kept a generous display of the latest issues from comic publishers Marvel, DC, Gold Key, Charlton, Archie, and Harvey, and we became frequent customers. The colorful comics sold for twelve cents each, and we used any excess change we could cajole from our parents to purchase the latest adventures of not only Batman but also Superman,

Spider-Man, the Flash, Captain America, Green Lantern, Iron Man, the Hulk, and any other hero who caught our fancy.

I already had developed a love for reading, so in a town that lacked a bookstore, comic books helped quench my thirst for exciting stories, with the accompanying artwork a bonus. Most of my friends put aside comic books by the time they reached junior high age, but I continued to read them well into high school. Over time, the stack of comic books in my bedroom grew, grew, and grew some more until it was multiple stacks on an old coffee table that one day collapsed from the weight.

> **I already had developed a love for reading, so in a town that lacked a bookstore, comic books helped quench my thirst for exciting stories.**

Fervent readers could find more to read within the pages than just the featured tales. In nearly all comics, we encountered advertisements for oddball items, such as sea monkeys or X-ray glasses. Stan Lee, editor at Marvel Comics, regularly penned a "Stan's Soapbox" feature in which he shamelessly promoted the company's work. On occasion, though, Stan grew serious and commented on societal issues, such as in 1968 when he derided bigotry and racism as "among the deadliest social ills plaguing the world today."

One comic book feature I read with a growing passion was the letters-to-the-editor page that appeared in nearly every DC and Marvel title. About four to six letters were printed each issue. Readers critiqued what they liked or didn't like about a previous issue's story or artwork, and on occasion the more astute scribes pointed out mistakes related to science, history, or general comic book story line continuity. These correspondents' names and hometowns appeared at the end of their letters.

I longed to have my thoughts, and my name, recorded on one of these pages, so one day at age eight or nine I penned a short letter sharing my views about a story in one of the Superman titles. It would be two to three months before DC published letters about this particular issue, so I had a torturous wait ahead of me. Finally, the banner day arrived, I bought the appropriate comic book and, ignoring that month's story, eagerly turned to the letters page to bask in my moment of glory.

My letter had not made the cut.

It was a heart-wrenching episode, but I valiantly carried on, vowing to put aside childish things such as mailing out missives from deep in the Appalachian Mountains to comic book editors in New York City. They probably detected my lack of sophistication and deemed me unworthy of a hallowed place on their pages.

And I did put aside such childish things as writing letters to comic book editors—at least until 1972, when I was fourteen.

One day, for reasons long forgotten, I gave comic book letter writing another try. This time I was older and wiser, and I understood that rather than sophistication, what I really needed was a strategy. The most popular comic books featured Spider-Man, Superman, Batman, and other superheroes, so I surmised competition for letter writers was fierce in those publications. It would be better to concentrate on a title where lack of interest could thin out the letter-writing herd.

I picked up the latest issue of a new title at the time, *Weird War Tales*, an unusual comic book that mixed combat with the supernatural. Audie Murphy meets H. P. Lovecraft, if you will. Perhaps, I figured, few readers bothered to write to this eccentric comic book. Maybe the editor, Joe Kubert, would print whatever plopped into his mailbox, happy to receive grammatically correct sentences that could fill the dreaded white space on the letters page and grateful that there existed a mountain-dwelling fourteen-year-old who owned a typewriter.

I began to type:

Dear Joe:

I have just finished reading Weird War Tales #5, and I thought it was great. Once again you have printed a comic that exceeds all others in this category. Your theme about escapes has been the best since this comic started. I especially liked "The Toy Jet."

At least it was succinct, if not particularly analytical. For a brief period around ages thirteen and fourteen I had shortened my first name from Ronnie to Ron, so I signed the letter "Ron Blair, Cumberland, Kentucky."

Letters about *Weird War Tales* no. 5 would not appear until issue no. 7, and since the comic was published bimonthly, that was four months away.

Once again, I waited.

On an otherwise forgettable July day in 1972, I entered the Rexall drugstore and raced straight for the comic book spinner rack. I understood enough about comic book publishing schedules to know *Weird War Tales* no. 7 should be among that day's arrivals.

It was. Here lay the moment of truth. I nervously opened the comic book as the clerks, cashiers, and other customers went about their business, unaware they were present at a potentially historic occasion.

I flipped to the letters page and scanned the signatures of that month's letter writers: Mark Colella, Glendale, California; Ed Leimbacher, Seattle, Washington; Matt Graham, Seattle, Washington; Ron Blair, Cumberland, Kentucky.

My strategy had worked. Intoxicated, I read my name again. And again. Then I read my brief letter, exulting in the moment. Years later, when I became a journalist, I produced thousands of bylined articles for daily newspapers. But these four dozen words in *Weird War Tales* no. 7 represented the first time something I wrote appeared in print.

Joe Kubert replied to all the letters, his responses appearing in bold type. Here is what he had to say to me:

Dear Ron:

The effort that goes into producing a comic such as Weird War**, beginning with the scripts, art, lettering, coloring, and winding up with the printing and distributing, is justified when comments such as your own are received.**

Only later did I notice the final letter on the page, which was a mere three sentences long. The signature: Unsigned, Somewhere, USA.

Unsigned? Someone had missed a golden opportunity to have his or her name dwell in eternal glory within the pages of *Weird War Tales*.

Inspired, over the next few years I wrote more letters, often churning out two to three a week. Not every comic book editor was as appreciative of my epistolary efforts as Joe Kubert, and most of those letters were fated to end up in the company of rats in some New York City trash bin. But perhaps two dozen or so achieved success, appearing in such titles as *House of Mystery, House of Secrets, Teen Titans, Shazam, Brave and the Bold, Monster of Frankenstein, Tomb of Dracula, Phantom Stranger*, and on one occasion the holy grail of letters pages—*Batman*. That was issue no. 247, in which I critiqued issue no. 244 by unleashing all of my fourteen-year-old overwrought prose on the comic book editors. Here is an excerpt:

The duel between Ra's al Ghul and The Batman was exciting and for once, no dialogue! Just dread silence in a fight that would mean someone's death. Talia, a girl with mixed emotions, could do naught but watch. Then the scorpion bite and our hero was left to die a death of suffering. No begging, though, for The Batman will grovel at no man's feet.

For good or ill, my words and name were now immortalized within the pages of a Batman comic book.

Sophisticated indeed!

CHAPTER 26

THE HOMESICK TRUMPETER BLUES

Life provides turning points in unexpected ways, and my family's move to the house on School Road when I was nine provided one for me. Next door lived "Junior" Sturgill, a teenager who played trumpet in the Cumberland High School marching band.

That same year, the high school band director visited Cumberland Elementary to tell us about plans for a beginning band program. I knew instantly I would join the band. I also knew what instrument I wanted to play—the trumpet, like my next-door neighbor, who was Herb Alpert and Al Hirt all rolled into one, at least in my admiring fourth-grade mind. Briefly, it appeared the band director might sabotage my plans, suggesting that the trombone would be a better fit for my lips. But I was adamant. He admired my allegiance to the trumpet, or perhaps surrendered to my obstinacy, and assured my mother that enthusiasm might outweigh mouth shape in this case.

Mom, accustomed to appeasing my whims, bought a used trumpet from a teenager who had upgraded to a better instrument. I waited impatiently as she boiled the mouthpiece to ensure I could practice my scales germ-free.

With three years of piano lessons behind me, I could read music, so I was ahead of the game there. Now it was simply a matter of learning which valves to press and how to tighten or loosen my lips to summon the appropriate notes.

Sadly, despite my music-reading abilities, I was no trumpet savant.

Sadly, despite my music-reading abilities, I was no trumpet savant, though for one brief delicious moment Mom believed I was. This was thanks to Junior. He hatched a prank that would showcase the talents of a high school trumpeter and transfer them to a novice who was satisfied to emit a sound—any sound—from the instrument.

Here is the scheme Junior outlined to me: I would stand, trumpet in hand, in front of a closed bedroom door. On the other side of that door, Junior would wait with his own trumpet. I would call to my mother, urging her to come listen to my first few days of trumpet progress. Then I would lift the trumpet to my lips and pretend to blow while randomly pressing valves. Behind the closed door, Junior would dazzle Mom with a song.

The prank worked to perfection, and Mom's eyes brightened as her musical-prodigy son demonstrated his magic. Perhaps she pondered contacting TV emcee Ed Sullivan to see if he had an opening for a nine-year-old trumpet soloist on his variety show that week.

The song ended, and Junior and I waited an appropriate amount of prankster time while Mom gushed about what a quick study I was. Then came the big reveal as Junior and his trumpet emerged. Mom, a good sport, laughed as much as we did, although perhaps beneath the mirth lay a smidgen of disappointment. The conversation with Ed Sullivan would have been so nice.

After a year of beginner band, I graduated to fifth-grade intermediate band. Then something extraordinary occurred.

The band director announced that a certain group of us in intermediate band—rising sixth, seventh, and eighth graders—now had acceptable talents to join the high school band. Yes, as a sixth grader I would take part in those high school football halftime shows as well as delight crowds at the town's annual Christmas parade. Maybe I was a savant after all. In retrospect, I suspect the band director had reached a moment of frantic desperation. Perhaps, while sketching out the halftime routine for the coming fall, he realized he lacked the proper number of bodies to accomplish his vision.

Regardless, it was quite the heady experience to be picked for high school band at age eleven. As it turned out, though, my introduction to my new, much older band mates was to be less than satisfying. This was through no fault of theirs.

Each summer, the high school band traveled two hundred miles to Camp Crescendo, a band camp in Lebanon Junction, a tiny town that drew its name from its position on the Louisville and Nashville railroad. The summer of 1969 would be no different, and early one morning I boarded a school bus that would take band members on the nearly four-hour journey to Camp Crescendo. As I took my seat, I harbored a secret I didn't dare share with the band director or the high school students. My mother knew, though, and she fought the urge to pull me off the bus and take me home.

My secret? I suffered from an acute case of homesickness. Even one night away from home, just a couple of blocks away at a friend's house, was too much to bear. Now I was about to spend an entire week half the state away.

I rode the bus in great despair, saying little if anything to the other band members as the miles ticked off and home grew farther and farther away.

When we arrived at Camp Crescendo, the girls headed in one direction and we boys in another to move into our housing for the week. Housing was a boot camp–style building with two rows of bunk beds. I climbed into a lower bunk, and a hefty teenager took the bed above me. The other teens expressed mock fear for my safety as the boy's mattress visibly drooped in my direction. This threat would hang over me all week, though as each night passed without catastrophe, I became more confident in the bed above's sturdiness.

That first evening at Camp Crescendo, it became obvious that I was an eleven-year-old in misery, longing for home and simultaneously feeling ashamed as I fought back tears. This would have been an opportune time for those teenagers to tease and taunt me unmercifully. That did not happen. Instead, one of the senior girls coaxed her boyfriend into taking me under his wing and keeping my spirits up. He faced quite the challenge, but throughout the week he and his pals made a valiant effort to help me fight my homesickness. To a reasonable degree, they succeeded, though I still suffered momentary bouts whenever a lull in camp activities happened.

Fortunately, the camp agenda allowed for few lulls. We practiced marching on a large field under the tutelage of a drill sergeant–style instructor who made it clear he would tolerate no shenanigans. One morning he kicked a teenager in the rear after the teen failed to perform a marching maneuver to his satisfaction.

Later, one high school student said to me, "Ronnie, if he kicked you like that, you would end up on the other side of the field."

This was true and funny, although not particularly reassuring.

When not marching, we practiced our music concert-style at an outdoor pavilion. Although marching was a new skill for me, I had played the trumpet for two years and felt confident anytime I had to pull the horn from its case and run through the scales. Yes, the high school students were more experienced and more skilled, but I held my own—except on the highest notes, which the older trumpet players accomplished with ease but I could not hit no matter how much I struggled to tighten my lips.

One morning we waited in the pavilion for practice to begin, and in the momentary downtime, my homesickness launched another attack. As I fought back tears, a pebble landed at my feet. Then another. I looked up to see the senior who had taken up the mantle as my temporary and sympathetic guardian.

"What's wrong?" he asked with a smile. It was a rhetorical question. He knew what was wrong. But his sympathy bolstered me, and that was my last moment of homesickness—at the camp or ever again.

Still, when the camp's final day arrived, I happily boarded that bus for the trip home. When, hours later, we rode past the sign that welcomed us to Cumberland, one of the teenagers started a song, and everyone joined in. It went like this:

Hurrah for Cumberland, hurrah for Cumberland,
Someone in the crowd holler hurrah for Cumberland.
One, two, three, four, who you gonna yell for?
Cumberland, that's who!

The town never looked so good as with great relief I returned home.

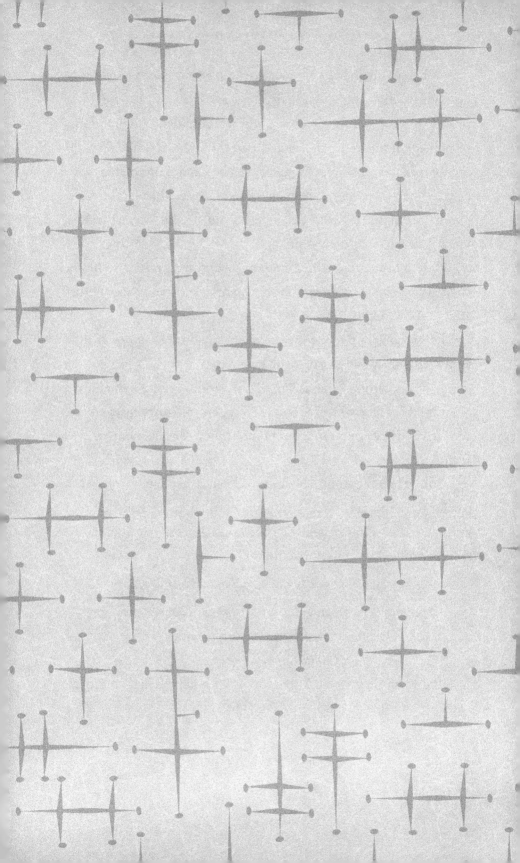

CHAPTER 27

COAL MINE, MOONSHINE, OR MOVE IT ON DOWN THE LINE

My senior year at Cumberland High School began in August 1975 and played out in fairly normal high school–senior ways. I donned shoulder pads and a helmet for a final season of football. I successfully applied to be on the yearbook staff. In English class we read Shakespeare's *Macbeth*, and in advanced biology we dissected a small shark, no doubt inspired by *Jaws*, the summer-blockbuster movie that captivated America in the months before the school year started.

In trigonometry we ... well, I'm not sure what we did in trigonometry, though I managed to finish the year with either an A or a B, mostly by memorizing formulas I only vaguely understood. In a pinch, trigonometry could have helped me measure the height of Black Mountain, although I found that looking up the height worked just as well.

But being a high school senior comes with pressures that have little to do with shark dissections or sines and cosines. In nine short months our teachers and parents expected us to walk across the gymnasium stage, accept our diplomas, and get on with the next chapters in our lives.

It was time to figure out what that next chapter would be.

For me, of course, it would involve college, because my parents had drummed that idea into me practically from birth. So, at a minimum, I had four years of study still ahead of me. The question was this: What would I study?

It was time to figure out what that next chapter would be.

I pondered career possibilities—teacher, lawyer—but kept coming back to journalist, the one job that seemed the best fit. I spent much of my spare time writing short stories, poems, plays, TV scripts, essays, or anything else where I could put nouns and verbs to work. But research told me it would be a daunting task to earn a regular paycheck with any of these forms of writing, at least right away, and while there was a bit of the romantic in me, I also had a strong practical side. A job as a newspaper reporter would allow me to write and put money in my bank account on a regular, predictable basis, even if the amount might be small. Journalism it would be.

As an aside, the year I graduated from high school, 1976, was also the year the movie *All the Presidents' Men* was released. The movie dramatically portrayed how two *Washington Post* reporters, Bob Woodward and Carl Bernstein, investigated the Watergate scandal and helped bring an end to Richard Nixon's presidency. On a few occasions, people would ask me if this inspired my career choice. The answer is no. I chose journalism knowing nothing about Woodward, Bernstein, or their investigative-reporting prowess.

The next trick was to choose a college. Originally, I expected to spend my first two years at Southeast Community College right there in Cumberland, then transfer to the University of Kentucky for the final two years. But the community college offered no journalism classes, which meant I would be a college junior before I could take the first course in my major. That could make graduating in four years problematic.

Maybe journalism wasn't the best option after all, especially since my parents' higher-education plan for us had always involved two years at the community college, where tuition was cheaper and we could avoid the added cost of a dormitory. I resigned myself to pursuing an alternative career path, likely as a high school English or history teacher. One day I made an offhand comment related to my future as a student at the community college.

Dad looked puzzled.

"I thought they didn't offer any journalism classes," he said. "Don't you need to find a college that does?"

My journalism journey was back on track.

As was the case with many high school seniors, my mailbox filled with college brochures. Predictably, most came from Kentucky colleges, but occasionally an outlier appeared. One day a brochure arrived from Culver-Stockton College, a private school along the Mississippi River in Missouri. I had never heard of Culver-Stockton and couldn't imagine why this obscure college would solicit obscure me, but I scanned its list of majors, and sure enough, journalism appeared. Briefly, I flirted with the notion of matriculating to this far-flung, mysterious locale 635 miles away, reinventing myself as a Missourian and enjoying the quizzical looks of my friends when they asked about my college plans. But practicality intervened once again, and I filed Culver-Stockton under the "I don't think so" heading.

If it sounds odd that I would give such a college more than a passing glance based on nothing more than a brochure, it wasn't. At least not completely. I was learning that many colleges didn't offer a journalism major, so any that did earned consideration, if only briefly.

Finally, three contenders emerged. They were, in order of preference, the University of Tennessee, Eastern Kentucky University, and Morehead State University. Tennessee lost its luster when the university informed me of the price of out-of-state tuition, and I eliminated Eastern Kentucky for other reasons. That left Morehead State. I applied, was accepted, and elected to attend without setting foot on the campus until new-student orientation a few weeks before classes began.

That seems like a roll of the dice now, but it proved a fruitful four years, as professors challenged me and I discovered like-minded people at the *Trail Blazer*, the weekly student newspaper that forced us to honor deadlines and learn to steel ourselves to critics who disparaged our work.

Back home in Harlan County, though, my career choice remained a puzzle.

"Journalism? There aren't many jobs for that around here are there?" a coal miner asked me one day.

"No," I agreed. "There aren't."

I had already determined I would not stay "around here." While I did start out as a reporter at the local *Harlan Daily Enterprise* (circulation seventy-five hundred), I eventually made my way to Florida, where journalism jobs flourished.

Perhaps such a migration was inevitable, or nearly so, regardless of my career choice. In *Coal Miner's Daughter*, a 1976 film about country singer Loretta Lynn's rise to fame, a character waxes philosophically, and a tad cynically, about Eastern Kentuckians and their employment prospects. He tells Lynn's husband, "If you're born in

Kentucky, you've got three choices: coal mine, moonshine, or move it on down the line."

I chose the last of these.

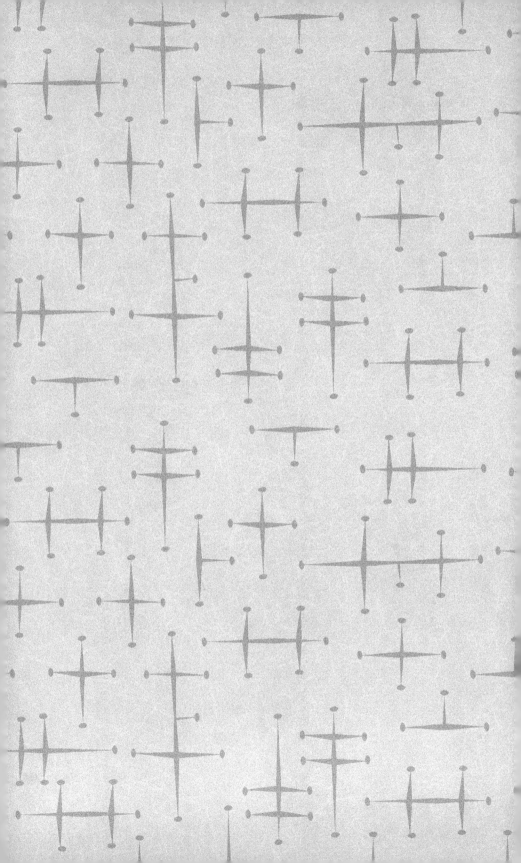

ACKNOWLEDGMENTS

Perhaps like many creative works, *Eisenhower Babies* did not always go in the directions I originally envisioned, and that's a good thing.

Delve far enough into childhood memories, and you realize there are missing pieces. The first five or six years are especially flimsy, almost like a movie trailer—several quick scenes that provide a disjointed glimpse that comes nowhere near to portraying the whole of the story. But as you struggle to craft random events into a crisp narrative, your mind grudgingly provides details previously forgotten or unveils lessons you didn't expect to learn.

Somewhere along the way, although this never fit into the final product, I came to appreciate the oddities of time and better grasped how it is one long flow rather than just isolated moments, as it can seem when you learn dates and events in history class. Here's a random example: on the day I was born, there were people still living who had been alive at the time of Lincoln's assassination.

Another thing you realize when writing a memoir is that you need assistance, and I had plenty.

I owe a special debt of gratitude to a number of people at Advantage Media who in some way championed the book or were instrumental in helping make it better. They include Mindy Cordell, Ben Douglas, Heath Ellison, Rachel Friedman, Josh Houston, Darryl LaPlante, Laura Rashley, Analisa Smith, and Adam Witty.

My sister, Shelia Blair Simpson, and my brother, Ricky Blair, reviewed a draft of the manuscript to help ensure my memories proved more or less sound and did not stray too far from the truth. My wife, Carol, a former newspaper copy editor with a sharp eye for ferreting out poorly structured prose, discovered errors, redundancies, and other problems too numerous to cite. She was amused—perhaps too amused—that my mother once dressed me as a girl for Halloween, and she prodded me for more details. Unfortunately, in this case my memory held tightly to its secrets and failed to produce enough specifics to satisfy her curiosity. Carol also pointed out portions of the manuscript where my narrative went astray, and she offered clear suggestions for getting clunkier passages back on track. Carol left the final manuscript in much better shape than she found it.

Memories, of course, go only so far, so plenty of research was involved, and a number of sources helped me sift through the backstory of the people, places, and events related to my childhood. For example, the US Census Bureau provided the figures about the number of US births during the Eisenhower administration, and a 1975 article from a medical journal, *Archives of Disease in Childhood*, informed me of mortality rates for breech babies in the 1950s. In many cases, I have cited my sources within the text.

My father's experiences in World War II proved to be one of the greater challenges, largely because he talked so little about the war, providing only brief snippets of information here and there that, on their own, would not total much more than a page. But I did have a copy of his army discharge papers that provided dates and locations for some of his movements between 1940 and 1945. By matching those with a few things he said, I managed to create a general narrative of his experiences. For example, Dad once told me that the one place he saw during the war that he would consider visiting again was Australia. But he never explained why he'd been in Australia. A little research revealed that by September 1943, Dad's Twenty-Fourth Infantry Division had relocated from Hawaii to Australia to begin training for what eventually would be their involvement in something called Operation Reckless in New Guinea. Sure enough, the discharge papers showed that Dad had participated in the New Guinea campaign.

Several sources helped me better understand my father's war experience by providing details about the events he participated in and what he likely encountered. Some of those sources include *Pearl Harbor Ghosts: The Legacy of December 7, 1941,* by Thurston Clark; *Day of Infamy,* by Walter Lord; *War at the End of the World: Douglas MacArthur and the Forgotten Fight for New Guinea, 1942–1945,* by James P. Duffy; *MacArthur's Jungle War: The 1944 New Guinea Campaign,* by Stephen R. Taaffe; and *Citizen Soldiers,* by Stephen E. Ambrose.

Finally, the most important acknowledgment is to my parents, Ellison and Jeanette Blair, who provided a stable home life, facilitated my reading and writing habits, insisted on hard work at school and at home, served as exemplary role models, encouraged me to explore varied interests such as sports and music, and made childhood a magical time.

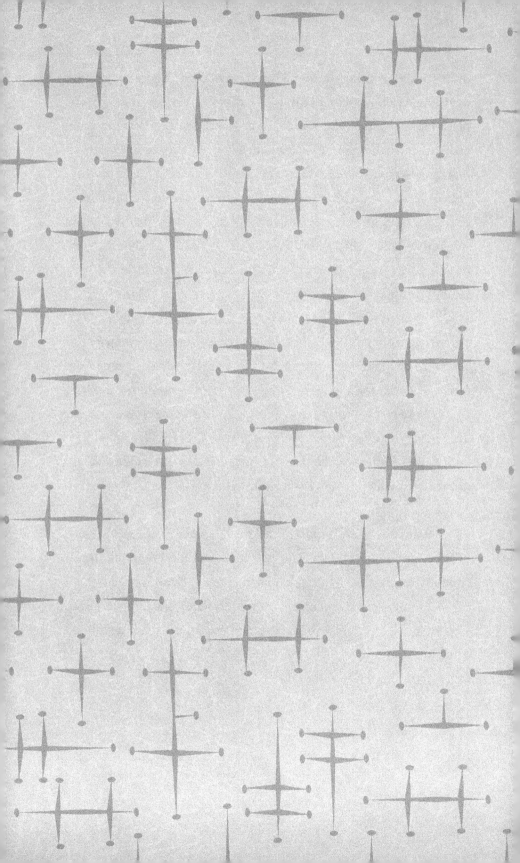

BIBLIOGRAPHY

Allen, Rick. "Remembering Six Gun Territory." *Ocala StarBanner.* December 28, 2010. https://www.ocala.com/story/news/2010/12/29/remembering-six-gun-territory/31426140007/.

Ambrose, Stephen E. *Citizen Soldiers: The U.S. Army from the Normandy Beaches to the Bulge to the Surrender of Germany.* New York: Simon & Schuster, 1998.

California Cable & Telecommunications Association Website, "History of Cable." https://calcable.org/learn/history-of-cable/.

Clark, Thurston. *Pearl Harbor Ghosts: The Legacy of December 7, 1941.* New York: Random House Publishing Group; Anniversary Edition, 2001.

Colby, Sandra L., and Jennifer M. Ortman. "The Baby Boom Cohort in the United States: 2012 to 2060," US Census Bureau, May 2014. https://www.census.gov/history/pdf/babyboomers-boc-2014.pdf.

Dreiser, Theodore, et al. *Harlan Miners Speak: Report on Terrorism in the Kentucky Coal Fields.* Harcourt, Brace & Co., 1932; Commonwealth Book Co., reprint, 2020.

Duffy, James P. *War at the End of the World: Douglas MacArthur and the Forgotten Fight for New Guinea, 1942–1945.* New York: Dutton

Caliber, 2016.

Florida Memory Website. "Chip Boyd with Baby Alligator Bought at Silver Springs, in His Yard in Panama City," 1962. https://www.floridam-emory.com/learn/exhibits/photo_exhibits/alligators/culture.php.

Fosl, Catherine, and Tracey E. K'Meyer. *Freedom on the Border: An Oral History of the Civil Rights Movement in Kentucky*. Lexington: University Press of Kentucky, 2009.

Grey, Zane. *Riders of the Purple Sage*. Forge, reprint, 2015.

Lord, Walter. *Day of Infamy*. New York: Henry Holt and Co.; Sixtieth Anniversary Edition, 2001.

Orwell, George. *The Road to Wigan Pier*. New York: Berkley Publishing Corp., reprint, 1961.

Raine, James Watt. *The Land of Saddle-Bags: A Study of the Mountain People of Appalachia*. Lexington: University Press of Kentucky, reprint, 1997.

Ralis, Z. A. "Birth Trauma to Muscles in Babies Born by Breech Delivery and Its Possible Fatal Consequences." *Archives of Disease in Childhood* 50(1) (January 1975): 5–13. https://adc.bmj.com/content/archdis-child/50/1/4.full.pdf.

Speciale, Christina. "Christmas Eve 1966 Snowstorm," WeatherWorks, June 11, 2015. https://weatherworksinc.com/news/1966-christmas-snowstorm.

Taaffe, Stephen R. *MacArthur's Jungle War: The 1944 New Guinea Campaign*. Lawrence: University Press of Kansas, 1998.

Weber, Bruce. "Peggy Charren, Children's TV Crusader, Dies at 86," *New York Times*, January 22, 2015. https://www.nytimes.com/2015/01/23/arts/peggy-charren-childrens-tv-crusader-is-dead-at-86.html.

US Department of Labor. "Analysis of Work Stoppages 1959," September 1960. https://www.bls.gov/wsp/publications/annual-summaries/pdf/work-stoppages-1959.pdf.

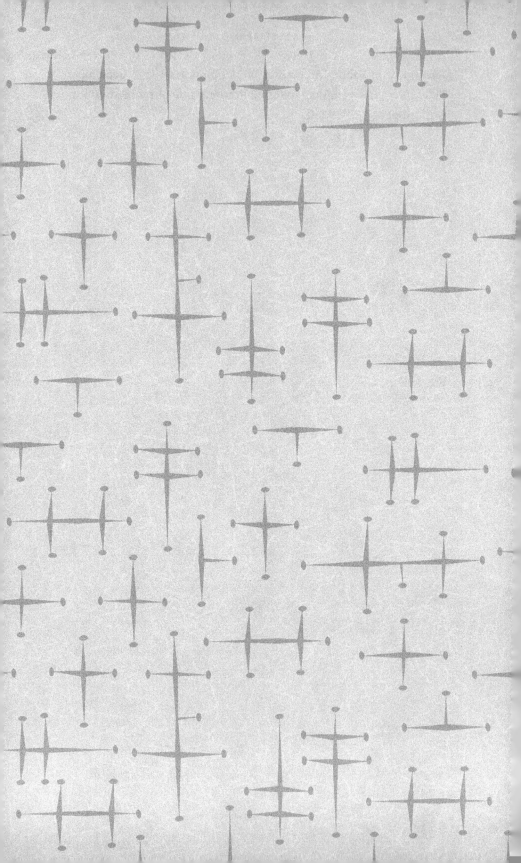

ABOUT THE AUTHOR

Ronnie Blair, a coal miner's son who grew up to become a journalist, is the lead writer for Advantage Media Group. Prior to joining Advantage, he worked for daily newspapers for more than three decades, including twenty years in writing and editing positions at the *Tampa Tribune*. During his newspaper career, Blair wrote about such varied subjects as education, business, crime, health, government, and many others. He holds a bachelor of arts degree in journalism from Morehead State University in his home state of Kentucky. He and his wife, Carol, have two sons, Alex and Andy.